HOW TO LIVE & WORK

In this Series

How to Be an Effective School Governor
How to Buy & Run a Shop
How to Choose a Private School
How to Claim State Benefits
How to Do Your Own Advertising
How to Employ & Manage Staff
How to Enjoy Retirement
How to Get a Job Abroad
How to Get That Job
How to Help Your Child at School
How to Keep Business Accounts
How to Know Your Rights at Work
How to Know Your Rights: Patients
How to Know Your Rights: Students
How to Know Your Rights: Teachers
How to Live & Work in America
How to Live & Work in Australia
How to Live & Work in Belgium
How to Live & Work in France
How to Live & Work in Germany
How to Live & Work in Spain
How to Lose Weight & Keep Fit
How to Make It in Films & TV
How to Master Book-Keeping
How to Master Business English
How to Master Public Speaking
How to Pass Exams Without Anxiety
How to Pass That Interview
How to Plan a Wedding
How to Prepare Your Child for School
How to Raise Business Finance
How to Raise Money for Community Projects
How to Run a Local Campaign
How to Start a Business from Home
How to Study Abroad
How to Study & Live in Britain
How to Survive at College
How to Survive Divorce
How to Take Care of Your Heart
How to Teach Abroad
How to Use a Library
How to Write a Report
How to Write for Publication

How To...

LIVE & WORK IN GERMANY

A Handbook for Short and Longstay Visitors

Nessa Loewenthal

Special Consultant
Alison Lanier

How To Books

British Library Cataloguing-in-Publication Data
Loewenthal, Nessa
  How to live and work in Germany. – (How to books)
  I. Title II. Series
  914.304

  ISBN 1-85703-006-0

© Copyright 1976 and 1977 by Overseas Briefing Associates
© Copyright 1983 by Intercultural Press, Box 700, Yarmouth, ME04096, USA
© Copyright 1990 by Alison Lanier

With additional material on education by Teresa Tinsley.

This fully revised and updated edition first published in the UK in 1991 by
How To Books Ltd, Plymbridge House,
Estover Road, Plymouth PL6 7PZ, United Kingdom.
Tel: Plymouth (0752) 705251. Fax: (0752) 695699. Telex: 45635.

All rights reserved. No part of this work may be reproduced (except for short extracts for the purposes of review), or stored in an information retrieval system without the express permission of the Publishers given in writing.

Typeset by Kestrel Data, Exeter
Printed and bound in Great Britain by
Dotesios Ltd, Trowbridge, Wiltshire.

Contents

1 Background 9

   Geography 9
   The people 14
   Famous Germans 15
   The government 16
   The current political scene 17
   Unification 19
   Economy 24
   Churches and religion 26

2 Before leaving 28

   Passports and permits 28
   Customs regulations 29
   What to take 31
   Getting a job in Germany 32

3 On arrival 36

   Money matters 36
   Time and dates 38
   Transportation 41
   Communications 43
   Language 46

4 Values and customs 49

   Conscientiousness 50
   Respect for the intellectual 50

Privacy	50
Formality	51
Handshaking	52
Manners	53
Time: Promptness	54
Friendship	54
Social customs	55
Conversation and personal style	57
Night life	58
Summary	58

5 Doing business in Germany 62

Language	62
Style	63
Business entertaining	64
Services available to UK businesses in Germany	65
Hierarchy in German companies	65
Summary suggestions	67

6 Household pointers 71

Housing	71
Electricity and appliances	74
Household help	78
Shopping	78
Measurements	82

7 Health and medical care 84

Health insurance	84
Spas	85

8 Education 86

International or local: it's your choice	86
German schools	89
English language schools	90
International Baccalaureate	92
Universities	93
Studying in Germany	94

9 Cars and driving	99
Speed limits and road signs	99
The big question: to import or buy locally?	100
Regulations	101
German automobile clubs	101
10 Adult leisure	103
Meeting Germans	103
Sports	104
The arts	106
Travel	107
11 Major cities	109
Bremen/Bremerhaven	109
Düsseldorf	111
Frankfurt am Main	112
München (Munich)	115
Bonn	117
German tourist information centres	120
Appendix: social security	121
Glossary	129
Further reading	133
Useful addresses	138
Index	141
Other titles in this series	143

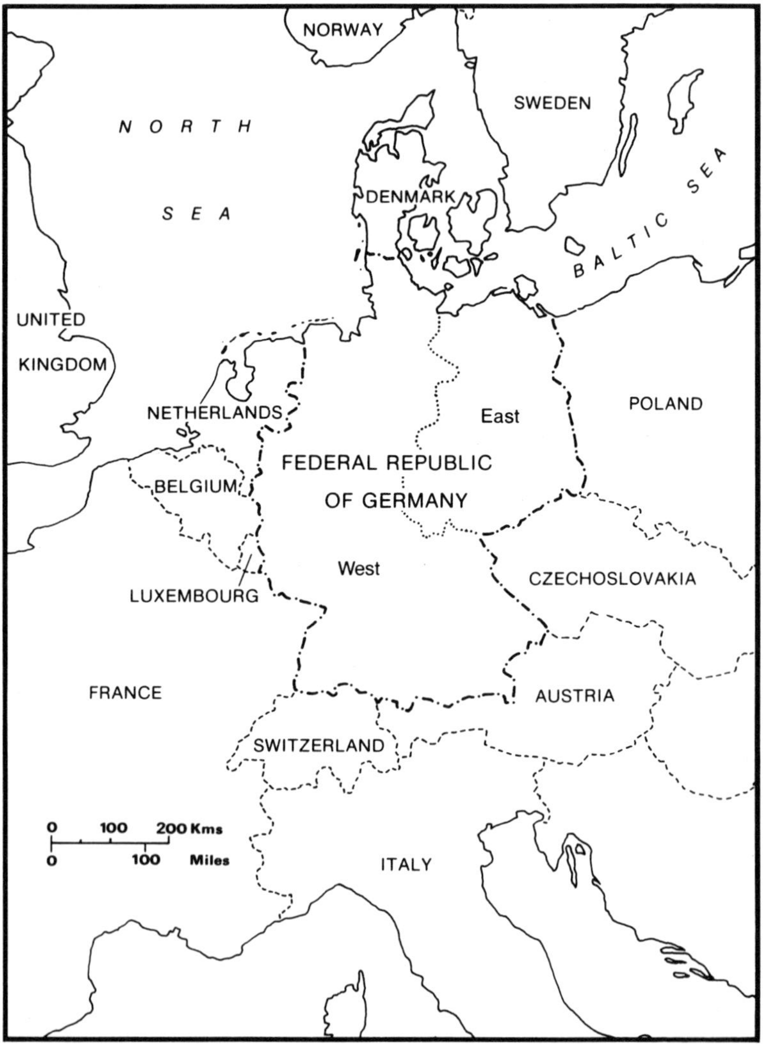
NORWAY
SWEDEN
N O R T H
S E A
DENMARK
BALTIC SEA
UNITED
KINGDOM
NETHERLANDS
POLAND
East
FEDERAL REPUBLIC
OF GERMANY
BELGIUM
West
LUXEMBOURG
CZECHOSLOVAKIA
FRANCE
AUSTRIA
SWITZERLAND
0 100 200 Kms
0 100 Miles
ITALY

1
Background

GEOGRAPHY

The Federal Republic of Germany (FRG) is not a large country. The area of the old West Germany, 96,000 square miles, was only slightly larger than the UK. What was East Germany was smaller, about 42,000 square miles. The new united Germany, with an area of about 138,000 square miles, is still considerably smaller than, for example, France (211,000 square miles).

The population of Germany is about 78 million (West Germany, 62 million; East Germany, 16 million)—as compared with 56 million in the UK and 55 million in France. After the Soviet Union, Germany has the largest population in Europe. Only the UK, Belgium and the Netherlands have higher population densities.

In West Germany, the population is very unevenly distributed. Almost a quarter of the population lives in villages of fewer than two thousand people while more than five million are concentrated in the three largest cities: Hamburg (1.6 million), West Berlin (1.8 million) and München (Munich) (1.3 million). Six smaller cities have populations topping a half-million each: Köln (Cologne), Essen, Düsseldorf, Frankfurt, Dortmund and Stuttgart.

In East Germany, about three-quarter of the population lives in urban areas. Apart from East Berlin (population just over 1 million), most large cities are in the south: Leipzig (563,000), Dresden (516,000) and Karl-Marx-Stadt (317,000).

Geographic regions
West Germany falls rather neatly into five main geographic regions: the north, the west or Rhineland, the Ruhr, Frankfurt am Main and Bavaria.

The north comprises a highly industrialised port area which includes the active seaports of Hamburg (Germany's largest city and most important port) and Bremerhaven, plus the major cities of Bremen, Kiel, Lübeck and Hanover.

The west or Rhineland, an area familiar to tourists, is bordered by Holland, Belgium, Luxembourg and France. Here lies the wide Rhine valley with its picturesque castles and vineyards—a main thoroughfare for freight-carrying river barges.

The Ruhr is the home of Europe's heavy industry, where Essen, Dortmund, Mülheim and other cities merge under smoke-laden skies, forming a densely populated magalopolis. On the nearby Rhine are Duisburg (Europe's largest inland port), Düsseldorf and Köln.

Frankfurt am Main and its southern neighbours, Stuttgart and Mannheim, form another prosperous industrial area. Frankfurt is the country's financial centre and the site of many trade fairs.

Bavaria is known worldwide for tourism, vineyards, wine and rugged mountain scenery; the music, spas, skiing and picturesque cities of the region, like München and Nürnberg (Nuremberg), delight its visitors. Although light and precision industries are concentrated in Bavaria, there is none of the heavy industry that is found in the north.

East Germany can be divided into two main areas. The south is generally hilly or mountainous, including the Thuringer Forest, the Erzgebirge (a mountain range forming a natural frontier with Czechoslovakia) and the Harz mountains which merge with West Germany in the south west. The central and northern regions form part of the vast North European plain—a low-lying area of heaths, lakes and marshes. East Germany is heavily industrialised. Major industrial centres are in and around East Berlin and the southern cities.

Even though Germany is a leading industrial nation, large areas of its land remain as pasture, cropland and forest—all in all, a pleasant and varied landscape. The industrialised areas are highly concentrated. Beyond them are medieval cities, vineyards, broad river valleys and old-world towns dominated by fortified castles, where one can forget the traffic sprawl and confusion of the major cities.

Rivers

Germany's rivers and canals form a superb water transport system, which is vital to commerce and connects the Federal Republic with the rest of Europe.

The Rhine, source of many a poem and song, is the greatest waterway, originating in Switzerland and emptying into the North Sea 537 miles away in The Netherlands. With its two main tributaries (the Moselle and the Main), the Rhine links south-west Germany to the Dutch Lowlands and the sea.

Three eastern rivers also flow into the North Sea and each has its port city: the Ems (Emden), the Weser (Bremen/Bremerhaven) and the Elbe (Hamburg).

In southern Germany the Danube flows 402 miles from west to east into Austria and Hungary, linking Germany to Central Europe and the Black Sea.

Connecting these large, natural waterways is a network of canals, of which the most recently constructed is the Rhine-Main-Danube canal, a shipping route that links the mouth of the Rhine in Holland with the mouth of the Danube in the Black Sea.

Climate

Germany's climate, although considered temperate, tends to be more rigorous than that of Britain. Usually the winters are colder (-10°C to 0°C (15 to 32°F) in January) and the summers hotter (about 20°C (68°F)) than we are used to. The climate becomes more continental the further east and south you travel.

Wherever you are in Germany, the weather changes frequently, even in the course of a day. Rainfall is consistent throughout the year, with cold winds in the winter. It seldom gets excessively hot; even in the summer, a warm sweater may be needed. Temperatures vary according to altitude and proximity to the sea. Snow falls frequently between December and March, and many of the higher areas from the Harz Mountains to the Alps are snow-covered all year. The wind-chill factor makes it seem even colder than the thermometer indicates because of the wind and the ever present dampness.

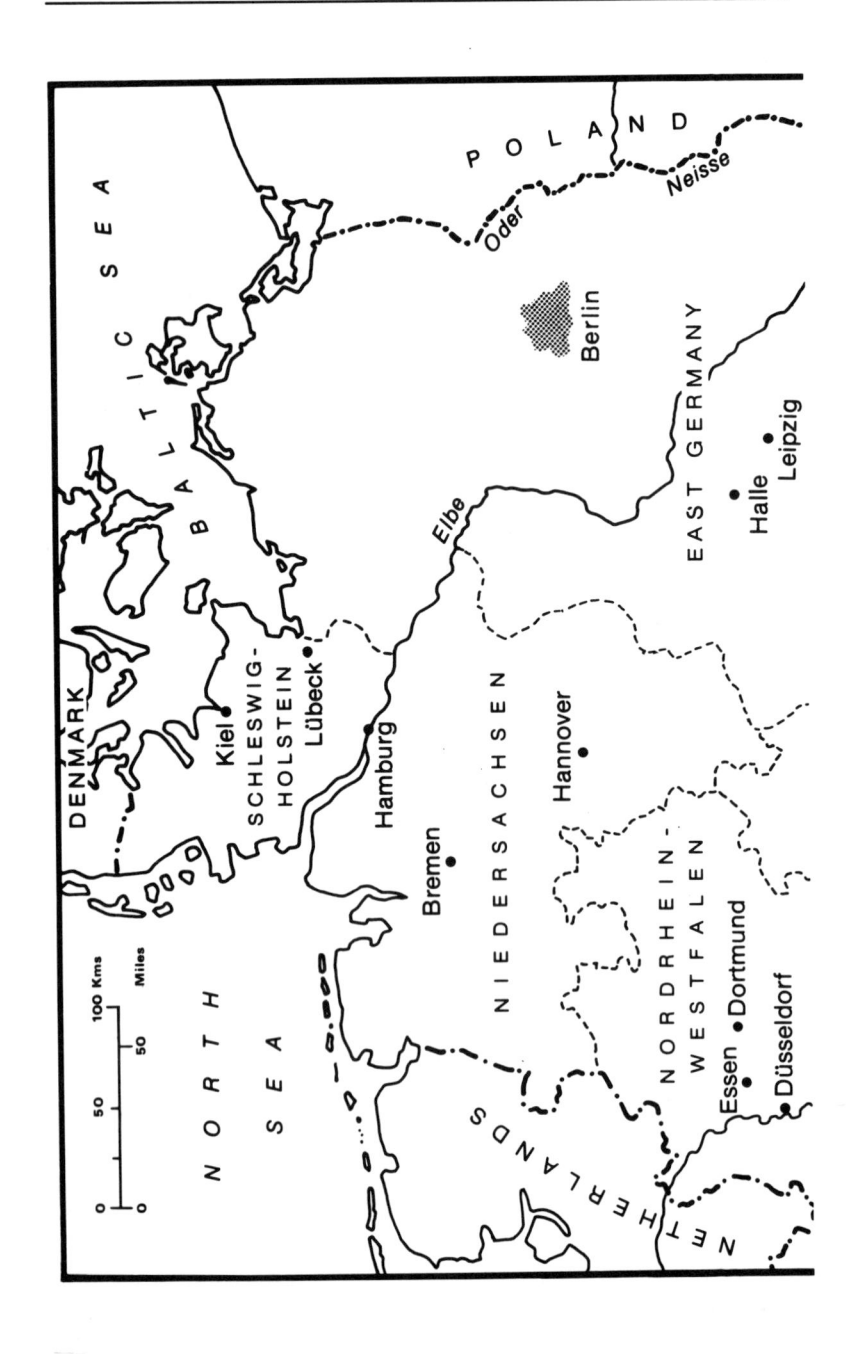
BALTIC SEA
POLAND
Oder
Neisse
Berlin
EAST GERMANY
Halle
Leipzig
Elbe
DENMARK
Kiel
SCHLESWIG-HOLSTEIN
Lübeck
Hamburg
Bremen
NIEDERSACHSEN
Hannover
NORDRHEIN-WESTFALEN
Dortmund
Essen
Düsseldorf
NETHERLANDS
NORTH SEA
0
50
100 Kms
0
50
Miles

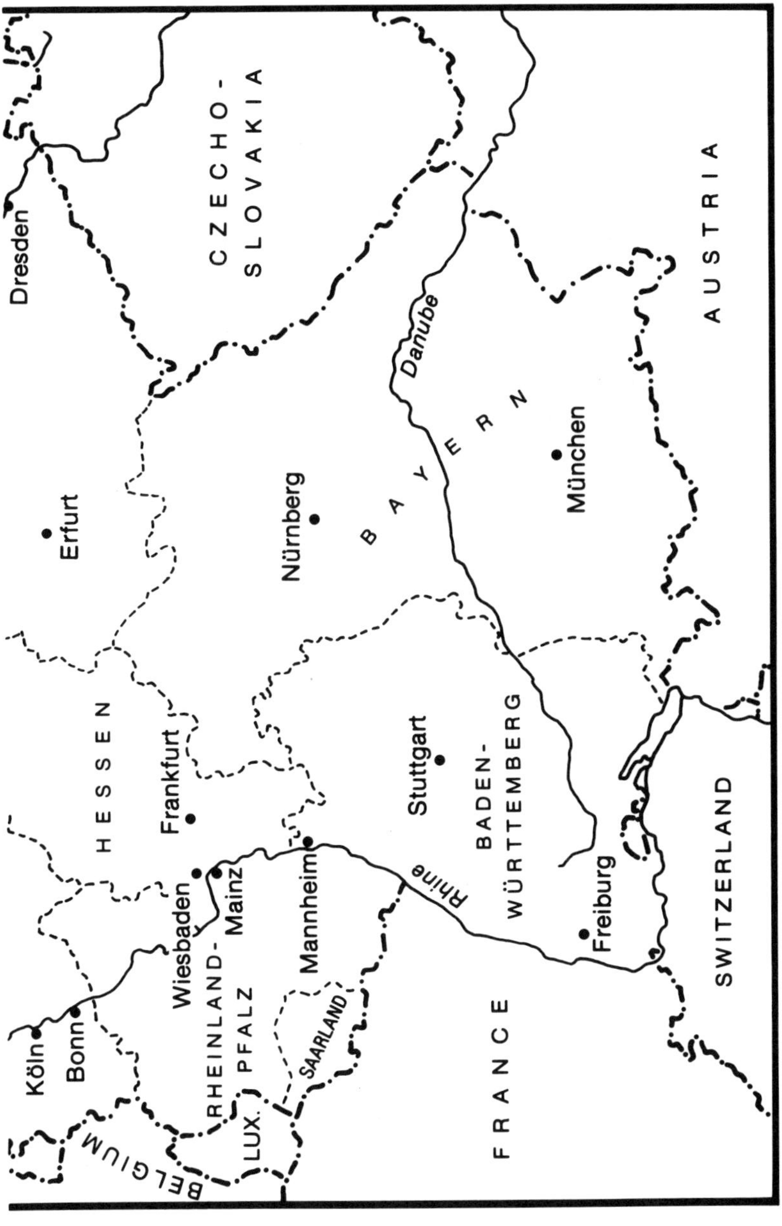
Dresden
CZECHO-
SLOVAKIA
Erfurt
Nürnberg
BAYERN
Danube
München
AUSTRIA
HESSEN
Frankfurt
Stuttgart
BADEN-
WÜRTTEMBERG
Köln
Bonn
Wiesbaden
Mainz
Mannheim
Rhine
Freiburg
SWITZERLAND
RHEINLAND-
PFALZ
SAARLAND
LUX.
BELGIUM
FRANCE

THE PEOPLE

Conservative, hard-working, formal and reserved, disciplined, clean, efficient, duty-bound—these are among the characteristics for which Germans are known. If this sounds drab, remember that Germans are also known for their ability to enjoy life fully, particularly with their families, around which most of their social life revolves.

The Germans share a common heritage, combining Teutonic strains (similar to those of the Scandinavians) with Latin and Slavic elements. And since Germany shares borders with nine different nations, there is an intermingling of cultures, especially along the frontiers.

In West Germany, society is dominated by its middle class, which prides itself on its ability to manage a densely populated land and a burgeoning economy effectively, a model of Western capitalism.

The population in the West recently reached 61 million people, with 646 people per square mile, even though the birthrate is low (0.2 per cent) and still declining. This crowding is partially the result of two major migrations since 1949, which added an estimated fifteen million people to the population: an influx of about thirteen million people from the eastern part of Germany and nearly four million *Gastarbeiter* (guest workers) from the south. (Added to this are the thousands of NATO troops—mostly from the United States—based in Germany.) By 1986 the number of foreign workers in West Germany had reached almost four million, even though since 1973 and the oil crisis, the inward flow of workers has been restricted almost entirely to nationals from other European countries: Turks, Yugoslavs, Italians, Danes, and Greeks. Several demographers predicted that because of the low birthrate, the population of the FRG by the year 2010 would be around thirty-five million, of which fewer than half would be of working age. This population crisis was one of the reasons why unification was greeted by many so enthusiastically (see further, below).

Whatever their nationality, all employees and their dependents automatically become members of the Federal Republic's social security system. To ensure that all foreigners employed by a German enterprise receive the many benefits to which they are entitled, the local social security office must be informed immediately of their employment. Social security agreements have been signed with other nations, including all EEC countries as well as most other Western European countries, the USA, Canada, Poland and Romania.

FAMOUS GERMANS

Every country has a roster of people to whom its inhabitants point with pride. Making such a selection for Germany is difficult because Germany has produced so many outstanding individuals that it is hard to select who should be included in such a list. Several have been significant not only in German history but in the development of Western culture as well.

Credit for publishing and mass literacy goes to Johann Gutenberg, who invented the first European printing press with movable type.

Others who changed history include Martin Luther, leader of the Protestant Reformation; two great philosophers, Immanuel Kant and Georg Hegel; and Albert Einstein, who formulated the theory of relativity.

There is a stream of great composers, including Johann Sebastian Bach, Johannes Brahms, Ludwig van Beethoven and Richard Wagner.

Among the greatest of Germany's many renowned authors are Johann von Goethe, Heinrich Heine and Heinrich Böll.

Albrecht Dürer and Hans Holbein rank with the greatest masters in art. Franz Marc and Max Ernst are significant in the development of modern art, and Walter Gropius is a well-known architect.

Two of Germany's greatest military and political leaders were Bismarck and Frederick II.

Wilhelm Roentgen discovered the X-ray; Robert Koch developed the tuberculin test; Hermann von Helmholtz applied the law of conservation of energy to mathematics; and Max Planck worked out the quantum theory in thermodynamics.

Even if you don't know about any of these people in great detail, you should be aware of their names and able to identify their major achievements. This will endear you to your German hosts, who will recognise and appreciate the fact that you are interested in them and have made an effort to learn about that which is important to them.

THE GOVERNMENT

The Federal Republic of Germany was established in 1949, when a constitution was drawn up by a consultative assembly of state representatives. Its Parliament is made up of two houses, the Federal Council (*Bundesrat*) and the Federal Diet (*Bundestag*).

The Bundesrat, which is the upper house of the Parliament, consists of forty-one voting delegates, each of whom has one vote, and four non-voting observers from West Berlin. Every state has at least three votes and the larger ones have up to five. Presidents of various *Länder* (who are automatically members of the Bundesrat) take turns serving as its president. Thus, all the Länder have direct representation at the federal level through this system of Länder government appointment and recall of delegates to the Bundesrat. The Bundesrat approves or disapproves legislation passed by the Bundestag.

The Bundestag, the lower house, is the principal legislative body, passing the laws and selecting the head of government. Its 496 voting representatives and twenty-two non-voting observers from West Berlin are elected to four-year terms by the people of their Länder.

The chancellor, who is also a member of the Bundestag, is elected by a majority of its members. He not only determines the general policy of the country but can also both propose and remove the federal ministers (who conduct the business of federal departments). Because of these roles, the chancellor is extremely powerful. Although the Bundestag does not have the power to remove federal ministers, it does have the power to remove the chancellor through a vote of no confidence; this acts as a control and balance of power within the government.

Technically, the head of state is the federal president, but he plays a very limited, mostly ceremonial role. For example, although he signs treaties and laws, they must be countersigned by the chancellor and by the federal minister concerned. The president is elected for a term of five years by a special Federal Assembly convened for that purpose, and he can be re-elected.

The federal government is responsible for such matters as national defence, federal finance, transport and communications. Diplomats are assigned by the Foreign Ministry, foreign policy is formulated by the chancellor and foreign minister, and treaties are negotiated by the Foreign Ministry or the ministry that has jurisdiction in the specific matters involved.

The Länder have control over education, cultural affairs, justice and public safety. Within each Land, local communes (neighbourhood councils) have considerable autonomy and the responsibility for administering their own affairs. Cities have a city council, mayor (*Bürgermeister*) and cabinet, all elected. Every municipality (*Gemeinde*) elects a mayor as well. Each county (*Landkreis*) elects a commissioner (*Landrat*) who is responsible to the state government.

THE CURRENT POLITICAL SCENE

After the Second World War, two key coalitions dominated the political scene in West Germany, one made up of the Social Democratic Party (SPD) and the Free Democratic Party (FDP), the other composed of the Christian Democratic Union (CDU) and the Christian Social Union (CSU). The latter (CDU/CSU) is now in power. At one time there was an effective coalition between the SPD and the CDU.

The general election in January 1987 confirmed the mandate of the coalition of conservatives (CDU) and liberals (CSU) to continue leading Germany. The federal chancellor, Helmut Kohl, retained a stable majority in the new Bundestag despite a considerable loss of votes for his party. Kohl's relative youth and length of service in the government convinced the public that he was sufficiently level-headed to provide competent and stable leadership.

In March 1987 the federal chancellor outlined for the Bundestag the principles and objectives of his government's policy for the next four years in three areas of concentration: home policy, Germany and foreign policy.

Home policy

The focus of the home policy is described as follows:

Freedom and responsibility together form the foundation of society, and awareness of these values must be sharpened. Without a legal order that is respected by all, there will be no free individual development or internal peace.

Protection of the environment is a major priority for the nation and is to be written into the constitution. A broad range of legislative and other measures is planned to ensure the preservation of the natural foundation of life—clean air and clean water. People have a right to live in a clean environment, but everyone must contribute through his or her own behaviour. Protection of the environment starts at home.

The social market economy is the best possible economic order to assure equality of opportunity, prosperity, environmental protection and social progress. Self-initiative and a spirit of enterprise are its foundations. They are indispensable prerequisites for successfully fighting the continuing problem of unemployment. Comprehensive tax reform is planned to ease the burden of the taxpayers and contribute to individual initiative.

Germany

FRG policy focused on the unity of the German nation and the preservation of the common national heritage. The government of the Federal Republic was committed to doing all it could to expand relations between the two German states, to create and maintain an open climate for communication, and to improve the contacts between the peoples of the Federal Republic and the German Democratic Republic. This policy has, of course, born fruit most dramatically in the recent events leading to the unification of the two Germanies (see below).

Foreign policy

The foreign policy of the Federal Republic of Germany is one of fostering global peace, and its security rests on the Atlantic Alliance. The political, economic and cultural future of the Federal Republic depends on a united Europe; therefore, the primary objective of its European policy is the further development of the European Community into a European Union. Its policy towards the Soviet Union is to work towards more understanding and cooperation—particularly in the field of disarmament and arms control—while guaranteeing the security of all.

Germany is an advocate for the development of the Third-World countries, viewing them as partners with equal rights whose drive for independence and self-determination must be supported. Aid to developing nations is considered a task of society as a whole that must involve private as well as government initiative and involvement.

UNIFICATION

Political unrest in the East

On 9 November 1989, a date which will be remembered and celebrated in history, the 'impossible dream' of German unity began to unfold as The Wall was first breached and then torn down.

The beginning of the end was the summer of 1989. Youthful East Germans, primarily intellectuals and professionals, disenchanted with the existing political, social, and economic realities of their lives, left the country on holiday, sought refuge in the Embassy of the Federal Republic of Germany in Hungary, and finally made their way to the FRG, entering as refugees. In September, members of the 'silent majority', who had previously talked only among themselves, decided to speak out. This group of intellectuals formed an organisation called the New Forum; they organised demonstrations and provided leadership to those in opposition to the communist regime. Jens Reich, one of the founders of the New Forum and a committed socialist, explained the new willingness to risk exposure and even life itself: 'You don't need courage to speak out against a regime. You just need not to care anymore—not to care about being punished or beaten . . . We reached the point where enough people just didn't care any more what would happen if they spoke out.'

Hopes and fears

In the early days of freedom, the question of unification with the 'other Germany' was accompanied by fear: fear that the 16 million people of the German Democratic Republic or GDR (East Germany), along with the country itself, would be swallowed up by West Germany; fear that the material and moral values of its egalitarian, collectivist society would be lost. There was also hope: hope for the future, hope for freedom of decision and of movement. Many East Germans crossed the border to reaffirm their hopes for change at home rather than in flight. One woman said she would go to West Berlin as a tourist, but 'our life is here. Besides, someone has to stay behind and change things. Everyone can't leave.'

The forced division of East and West Germany is a thing of the past, but the problems inherent in creating a new union are becoming apparent and are a cause of concern—particularly to the East Germans, who must bear most of the burden of change. In the process, citizens from both East and West are becoming aware of the differences between them, which may take years to overcome —if they are overcome at all.

The euphoria initially experienced by both sides has disappeared as the realities of everyday life become evident, generally expressed in terms of loss and/or fear. In an effort to quiet people's fears, the East German leadership issued an appeal to the population to develop a society of solidarity in which peace and social justice, individual freedom, freedom of movement, and the preservation of the environment are guaranteed. Egon Krenz, former Prime Minister, committed the government to rehabilitating socialism with a heavy dose of democracy and environmentalism.

In the Federal Republic, dreams of unification compete with the fear of political and life style changes. These fears and concerns continue despite reassurances offered by Chancellor Kohl and the Christian Democratic Union (CDU). In September 1989—before the fall of the wall—the unemployment rate was 7.5 per cent, and housing shortages already existed in all major cities. The influx of the East Europeans, including East Germans, is causing concern about the future direction and leadership of the Federal Republic; polls reveal that the East Germans and other immigrants/refugees tend to favour the more conservative ideas of the Nationalist and Christian Democrats over those of the Social Democratic party.

The rush towards unity
This last factor was probably the reason for the speed with which unification was accomplished. Chancellor Kohl badly wanted to be known as the first chancellor of a united Germany. In an effort to benefit from the conservative leanings of the East Germans, he brought forward the date for economic unification to July 1990. A Frankfurt paper summarises the views of many in the East and West: '. . . The train of German unification is moving so fast that at times it seems to have arrived before departure times have even been announced . . .'

Following a visit by Kohl to the Soviet Union for talks with President Gorbachev, all remaining political and diplomatic obstacles to unification were removed. On 3 October 1990 East Germany ceased to exist. In December 1990, Kohl's Christian Democrats won the largest share of the votes in the first German-wide election held since 1932. Germans had overwhelmingly endorsed unification.

A threat to Western peace?

Unification was seen by many in Europe and the West as a threat to peace. The leaders of these nations have long felt that the stability of Europe rested on two German states—one tied to the East and one to the West. There was also fear that unification would be the beginning of the Fourth Reich, the rebirth of 'The Fatherland'. This is a fear that both West and East Germans want to lay to rest. There is no thought, in the minds of the leaders, of reviving the German nationalism that existed from 1871 to 1945. When Germans look back at that period, they see war, death, delusion and tragedy. This retrospective perception explains why most Germans are not thinking about redrawing maps.

The population crisis

There was also a positive, practical perspective to unification—West Germany needed immigrants. Its population was stagnant and aging rapidly. Demographic forecasts showed that it would lose 10 per cent of its population in the next thirty years. This trend has already been felt—in 1989, 200,000 apprenticeships went unfilled. Those companies which have taken advantage of the recent influx of Eastern European refugees feel that they add dynamism to the economy and to society at large, that they are highly reliable and quickly become productive members of the workforce. In fact, FRG government economists are predicting that the current burden of resettlement will be quickly repaid by the income produced from social security and income tax payments from this new addition to the workforce.

Economic unification

When the supporters of the New Forum dreamed of (and marched for) freedom and unity with West Germany they were driven more by economics than by politics. They were seeking better jobs, more discretionary income, and higher living standards—what some called 'Mercedes democracy'. East Germany will quickly become an important part of the Federal Republic's economy because it is a source of low-cost labour and provides a ready market for products. Along with economic unification are problems which must be recognised and dealt with: unemployment due to the closing of plants and cutbacks in military forces; the need for East Germans to pay for services and necessities which had been provided at a controlled cost—mortgages, rent, heat, bread;

concern about job security; and the realities of inflation and higher taxes.

In spite of the problems, there is hope in the East. Thousands of new companies and businesses have been registered; several American and European subsidiaries have established themselves, utilising facilities formerly occupied by government-owned cartels; and West German firms ranging from banks to construction companies are rushing to establish businesses or joint ventures. The Federal government has committed large sums of money to assist in undoing the damage to city infrastructures, housing and the environment resulting from forty years of neglect.

Social unification

The fact that three-quarters of the East Germans believe that the state is, and should continue to be, responsible for their welfare is an indication of the problems involved in social unification. In order to meet the needs of those who hold this perception, the social policies of the new Germany must be changed. There are also strongly differing perceptions of individual responsibility for the environment, for the overall quality of life, and for the role of the individual as a member of society.

Cultural unification

George Kennan describes 'romantic linguistic nationalism' as a belief that a common language creates a community. Many observers feel that the Germans have subscribed to this point of view for more than a century and that, in fact, cultural unification will remain a myth, that the creation of one culture from many—if possible—will take at least three generations to achieve. The shared values of the two Germanys are those espoused by Luther and Goethe. Many of the differences between the two societies are political and economic and will change over time, but the deeper the value, the greater the difference.

It is interesting to note that the East German fits the stereotype of 'The German' much more closely than does the West German. It is the East German who is spartan, puritanical, innocent, and who lives in a homogeneous society. In West Germany, during the forty years of separate existence, many traditional 'German' biases have disappeared. The West German of today is more European than German, according to Elizabeth Boelle-Neuman of the Allensbach Research Institute. 'We care about the Third World and the environment. We have a peace movement. We value opposing views.'

Irene Runge, an East German sociologist, says: 'Decades of socialism have reinforced our worst traits. We East Germans are more respectful of authority, less flexible, and less accepting of individual differences than we were before the war.' In East Germany, as in most of the Eastern Bloc countries where nationalism has been repressed, nationalistic groups are beginning to reappear. Runge continues, 'Xenophobia runs deep among East Germans. We will not make very good democrats.' Visitors to the cities report being surrounded by skinheads shouting, '*Auslander raus!*'

A European perspective

No one can predict what will happen, or when, but whatever happens in the process of unification, there is agreement on the part of the Federal Republic and other Western nations that the German situation needs a European solution; that, as a collective European issue, change can be managed peacefully and in the best interests of all. The Foreign Ministry of the Federal Republic explained that its goal is 'to bring about West European integration . . . with the idea that the German question will solve itself within a confederated Europe'. It is also apparent that the stability of each nation and of Europe is a primary concern.

The dream of a unified Germany has been kept alive through the years by the hope of a new and united nation—living in peace with each other and with its neighbours. This new Germany is described by Helmut Kohl as 'embedded in the European security architecture,' and as a 'transit point for ideas and perspectives between the East and the West.' The realisation of this dream depends on the ability of Germany's leaders to bring the economy of East Germany in line with that of the FRG.

Managing change

The opportunities and challenges available to European and FRG businesses are being recognised and acted upon, but it is essential that those involved also recognise that changes must meet the needs of the East Germans, that change doesn't occur overnight, and, if forced, it will be costly and ineffective over the long run.

It is also critical that the differences in deep-seated attitudes and values, in perceptions and behaviours be recognised, accepted, and respected. In order to function effectively and to succeed in today's global economy, those involved in interactions with people from other cultures need to be aware of the existence of these differences and prepared to accept the challenge of working with them.

ECONOMY

In the aftermath of the Second World War, Germany lay in ruins. It had been defeated politically and militarily, much of its industry had been destroyed, and its economy was in a state of chaos. It is now the dominant economic power in Europe—so much so that many Europeans are both wary and envious. Having weathered the economic ups and downs of the 1970s and 1980s, Germany is today the world's leading exporter of manufactured goods and has one of the world's most stable currencies.

The FRG trades extensively within the European Community, of which it is one of the original members, and with the rest of Europe and the United States. It accounts for almost 10 per cent of total world trade and is the second largest trading nation after the USA. Germany is Britain's largest trading partner. In 1986, Britain's exports to the Federal Republic amounted to 12 per cent of total British exports worldwide, and were second in volume only to British sales to the United States.

The German middle class is stable and has greatly expanded in recent years due to the general prosperity, generous employment benefits, and tax credits for home ownership (40 per cent of Germans are home owners).

Most people are employed in business and industry or in public service. Only about 15 per cent work in agriculture and related industries or are self-employed. Thus, when the business economy suffers, there are severe repercussions. The standard of living has risen dramatically since 1950, but all Germans now feel the pressure of increasing inflation. The rapid economic growth of the 1970s has recently fallen victim to an economic slowdown and to vigorous competition from Japan in the sale of manufactured goods. The gross national product, on the rise for all of the 1970s, is falling, and West German spirits are sagging with the statistics.

Labour-related issues are among Germany's thorniest problems. And one of those issues is the very generous benefit package that German workers have obtained through social legislation (see Appendix I). Illness is compensated by full wages for six weeks and 75-80 per cent thereafter from health insurance funds. Nearly everyone is covered for major medical and dental costs. Pension plans are written to include adjustments for both inflation and the rising average wages of fellow workers, and are available for self-employed people, including housewives. For the first year, unemployment benefits equal 68 per cent of a worker's salary, and welfare benefits total 58 per cent of former pay. Holiday benefits are also very liberal. But those benefits take a large bite out of the workers' pay and impose a heavy burden upon both business and government. The social programmes, once affordable, are now the albatross around the German neck.

A second labour issue is unemployment, which, at over 10 per cent, is the worst since the postwar years. Labour problems are a national disease and are slowly sapping strength from the German economy. In the late 1960s a shortage of labour led to the recruitment of large numbers of foreign workers who, together with their families, now account for almost 7 per cent of the German population. In 1973 recruitment of foreign labour except from European Community countries was banned in an effort to relieve the strain on the economy. All EC workers and all other foreign workers holding work permits have the same legal status as their German colleagues.

Worker participation
Germany has moved, more than most societies in the free world, in the direction of worker participation. The Shop Organisation Act of 1972, which applies to all businesses employing five or more persons, provides a variety of rights of codetermination both in social and personnel questions.

For example, in large companies with five hundred or more employees, one-third of the directors must be representatives of the employees (except in the coal and steel industries, where half the supervisory board must be employees). In addition, even in small firms there is a Works Council, which further represents the interests of the workers vis-à-vis the employer.

As one might expect, trade unions are strong in Germany. About seven million workers are members of the largest one, the German Union Federation (*Deutscher Gewerkschaftsbund* or DGB), which actually comprises sixteen individual trade unions. The salaried, white-collar technical and public service employees have professional associations of their own, such as the German Civil

Servants Association (*Beamtenbund*), German Salaried Employees Union (*Deutsche Angestellten-Gewerkschaft* or DAG), and the German Armed Forces Association (*Bundeswehrverband*). Trade unions and employer associations negotiate agreements on working conditions without the involvement of the state. Usually, they are successful in their efforts; however, the workers' right to strike and the employers' right to lockout are available as ultimate expedients. Basically, these rights of protest (union) and self-protection (employers) encourage negotiation and are the foundation of the harmonious labour-management-government relations. This balance of cooperation and autonomy is also the basis for Germany's extremely high productivity and for the strength of the agreements made between labour and management.

CHURCHES AND RELIGION

The relationship between church and state in Germany is rather different from that in Britain. Churches in Germany are supported by an 8-10 per cent tax on income. This tax is collected by the internal revenue office and distributed to two church administrations: the *Evangelische Landeskirche*, composed of Lutheran and Evangelical churches, and the Catholic Church.

The funds are used to maintain and construct church buildings, compensate the clergy, and support religious observances. The funds are also used to operate institutions such as hospitals, nursing homes, schools, kindergartens and day-care centres. Smaller groups, including the Baptists (*Freie Kirche*), Methodists and Jehovah's Witnesses receive support from voluntary, tax-exempt contributions of members. Members of other religious groups, atheists, and those who have officially dropped their church affiliation are not required to pay the church tax.

Christianity as a religious preference predominates in the Federal Republic; about 49 per cent of the population are Protestant; almost 45 per cent are Roman Catholic. Less than 1 per cent are Jewish. About 40 per cent attend church regularly. Protestantism tends to be stronger in the north and Catholicism dominates in parts of the Rhineland and in the south.

Because so many state-related services involve the church, connections with the church are useful if you wish to function in German society and make social connections. Each parish contains roughly 3,500 people, and the pastor has specific duties to carry out within his or her parish and may be involved in activities ranging from organising and leading tours and teaching religion in the schools to conducting weddings and funeral services and visiting the sick. Pastors are engaged in the secular and ceremonial life of the community to a remarkable degree. Courses in religion are taught in the schools, but parents may request that their child be exempted from religious instruction. Children over the age of fourteen can decide to eliminate religion from their course of study.

2
Before Leaving

PASSPORTS AND PERMITS

For entry into the Federal Republic a national of an EC country needs a passport but not a visa. Nor are immunizations required in many cases. Nevertheless, you may want to obtain an international health record card on which to keep personal health information.

In order to work or look for work, a UK citizen needs a **full British passport**; a visitor's passport is not sufficient. EC citizens do not require a work permit to work in Germany, but all foreigners need a residence permit—this applies to each member of the family, even an infant. This residence permit or *Aufenthaltserlaubnis* will be documented in your passport. Although it is best to get this permit in advance through a German consulate, it is possible to obtain one in Germany if you apply for it within three months after arrival at the Aliens Authority (*Ausländeramt*) at the regional police office nearest to you. The permit is usually valid for five years but may be renewed.

Within a week after your arrival in the Federal Republic, you must register with the community or mayor's office of your locality. Hotels do this for their guests, which is why they usually collect your passport when you check in and keep it overnight. When you rent a house or flat, you must complete the same registration form, and when vacating your living quarters, you must file a report within one week. You will also need a Tax Card, which is obtained from the district tax office.

This may seem like a lot of paperwork and red tape, and you may find it irritating at times if you are not used to it. Germany is simply a thorough, deliberate and careful society; as a guest, it is necessary to live within the system.

CUSTOMS REGULATIONS

When entering the Federal Republic from an EC country, individuals may take the following items duty-free, but they must be hand carried or in accompanying luggage (they should not be shipped with household goods). All items should be for personal use only.

- 200 cigarettes (300 if not bought in a duty-free shop) or 75 cigars or 400 g tobacco.
- 1 litre of spirits more than 22 per cent proof (1.5 litres if not bought in a duty-free shop), *or* 3 litres of spirits less than 22 per cent proof.
- 5 litres of wine.
- 75 g perfume and 1/3 litre of toilet water.
- other goods to the value DM 780.00 (easiest if these are hand-carried).

All tobacco and alcohol allowances are for those aged 17 or over. Smokers will probably want to take their maximum allowance as tobacco prices are high.

Different allowances apply if you are arriving from outside Europe or from a non-EC European country.

Import of household goods

Household goods may be imported into Germany without payment of customs duty or border tax on presentation to the German customs authorities of reasonable proof of the following:

1. You have given up your previous residence abroad (eg, documents showing the termination of your lease and/or employment or the sale of your residential house); or you have been transferred to Germany by your employer. Maintaining two residences (that is, keeping your residence at home) does not necessarily result in a denial of customs exemption if you are also establishing a new German residence.

2. You are establishing a residence in Germany (ie, a lease,

correspondence with your employer, German police registration receipt.)

Customs exemption is granted *only* for goods that you have been using personally or professionally abroad and which you intend to use again in Germany. Food and similar perishable items are restricted to quantities normally stored at home. Alcohol and tobacco products are not permitted duty-free except for the amount you are allowed to carry with you when entering the country (see page 29).

A motor vehicle that was registered in your name(s) as the sole owner(s) at your previous place of residence may also be imported to Germany duty-free, provided you have a registration certificate from your previous motor vehicle licensing authority. Although there is no minimum requirement for the length of time of your ownership, German customs must be satisfied that you are importing it for personal use only.

Before they can be licensed, cars must pass inspection by the German Technical Inspection Team, and cars of foreign manufacture may have to undergo certain modifications to conform to existing German requirements. Since this can be rather expensive, it is usually less costly to bring in only relatively new cars (for more information on import or purchase of cars, see chapter 9).

All household goods should arrive at approximately the same time as you arrive in Germany. If that is impossible, the goods should arrive as soon as possible after you enter the country. If you declare personal belongings on arrival, you will have a three-year time limit for receiving the goods. A detailed description of the contents of your shipment must be presented to customs officials when you arrive, even if your shipment will not be arriving for many months.

This information is included only as a general guide. The German Customs Office will ascertain whether the effects to be imported are reasonably consistent with your personal, professional and economic status. Special rules govern items such as guns, rifles, ammunition and machines used to produce them, certain pets, and plants. More detailed information can be obtained from the nearest German consulate or from the German Embassy.

When you leave Germany, you may export your household goods freely, with no limitations on food, alcoholic beverages, or tobacco products. You need, however, to be concerned about the regulations at your next destination.

Importing pets
Germans are pet lovers, so if you decide to take your pet(s), you will have a minimum of difficulty. Dogs, if well behaved, can usually be taken on trains (an extra fee is charged on first-class trains) and are often permitted in hotels and even restaurants. Vets are excellent, and you will find every kind of food and equipment for almost any animal or bird.

If you bring a dog or cat into Germany, you must have the animal vaccinated against rabies within ten days prior to your entering the country, and you must also present a notarised German translation of the vaccination certificate. In addition you must provide a health certificate or a letter written on the vet's stationery stating that the animal is in good health. This letter or certificate must be written in German or accompanied by a translation, and it must:

1. state the name, breed, colour, sex, and age of the animal;
2. be prepared at the point of origin within ten days of the pet's arrival date; and
3. attest to the non-occurrence of rabies within a thirteen-mile radius of the pet's home within the past three months.

For your own protection, have your pet inoculated for all possible diseases. If your pet regularly takes any medication, you should carry a supply with you, along with a letter from the vet naming the medication and describing the reason for its use.

Arrangements for your pet's transportation should be made with the airline as far in advance as possible because the number of animals the airline can carry on a flight is limited. Most airlines, with sufficient notice, will provide an appropriate animal carrier. Lufthansa and KLM have particularly good 'Jet-Pet' service. If you provide your own carrier, make sure it is approved by the airline prior to your departure. Also, check with your vet for medication (relaxant or tranquilliser) which will make the trip easier for your pet.

WHAT TO TAKE

Although Germans are becoming increasingly casual in dress, they are generally quite concerned about dressing appropriately. Throughout Europe, people dress well in public and would not, for example, wear shorts or bright sportswear on city streets.

Germany's cool climate dictates your wardrobe to a large degree. Winters are cold and damp; in the north the wind blows off the sea and the fog rolls in frequently. Even in the summer, it seldom gets excessively hot, so generally warm clothing is recommended. Bring windproof jackets, pile-lined or down coats, and warm nightwear since houses are often chilly. Sturdy rainwear (raincoats with zip-out linings are handy) and boots are necessities.

Men will need the usual business clothing: suits, shirts and ties of the same weight as would be appropriate in most cold climates. Sports clothes will be useful as well. Both men and women should take a good supply of shoes since German shoes are sized differently (see p. 82), making it hard to find shoes that fit. If you are able to find a fit, you will find that German shoes are well made and quite reasonably priced. Be sure to bring sturdy walking shoes for the cobblestone streets and for sightseeing.

Women wear wool most of the year—suits, wool dresses or trousers (which are worn a great deal), warm hats, and a winter coat. Take tights and underwear since they, like shoes, are sized differently. Also, bring one or two cocktail dresses and possibly a long dress since German social occasions are often quite formal.

In comparison to adults, young people tend to dress very casually. Children and teenagers wear blue jeans and T-shirts. You will notice that many teenage girls wear small purses around their necks (not over the shoulder) because they are convenient and less likely to be lost or snatched. Clothes of all kinds are available for young people and for infants and children, as are terry and disposable nappies.

You can buy almost any type of clothing you might want or need. High-priced coats and suits are excellent and well styled, but medium-priced clothing, although well made, tends to be designed more for German tastes.

For information on household appliances, see chapter 6.

GETTING A JOB IN GERMANY

The employment market in Germany is dominated by the Federal Institute for Labour, or *Bundesanstadt für Arbeit* based at Regenburgerstrasse 104, 8500 Nürnberg. It has more than 600 main and branch offices (*Arbeitsamt*) throughout Germany; private employment agencies such as Manpower and Adia account for relatively little of the employment market. The Institute has a central placement service (*Zentralstelle für Arbeitsvermittlung*), at Feuerbachstrasse 42-46, 6000 Frankfurt-am-Main, which can be of particular help to applicants from overseas, who should apply to the *Auslandsabteilung* (overseas department). The publications of the Zentralstelle include *Markt und Chance* (a weekly jobs bulletin) and *Uni*, a free jobs magazine targeted at students.

As far as advertised vacancies are concerned in the press, the leading newspapers to look at are:

Frankfurter Allgemeine, Hellerhofstrasse 2-4, 6000 Frankfurt-am-Main
Süddeutscher Zeitung, Sendlingerstrasse 80, Munchen 8.
Die Welt, Kolnerstrasse 99, Bonn.
Die Zeit, Postfach 106820, 2000 Hamburg.

A good all-round starting point is another book in this series, *How to Get a Job Abroad* by Roger Jones, 2nd edition 1991 (How to Books Ltd, Plymbridge House, Estover Road, Plymouth PL6 7PZ).

Work camps and community work
Organised mainly for younger people, there are a number of work camps held each year all over Germany, offering the chance to combine a German living experience with useful activity. The main ones include:

Aktion Sühnezeichen/Friedensdienste e.V.
Jebenstrasse 1, D-1000 Berlin 12.
Intended for applicants aged 18 or over, and willing to spend 18 months on projects involving social work with children, the handicapped, drug addicts and other groups.

Arbeitsgemeinschaft der Evangelischen Jugend in der Bundesrepublik und Berlin e.V.
Porschestrasse 3, D-7000 Stuttgart 40.
Minimum age 18. Applicants with a basic command of German are placed in international work/study camps.

Arbeitskreis Freiwillige Soziale Dienst Stafflen

Stafflenbergstrasse 76, D-7000 Stuttgart.
German-speaking applicants aged 18 to 25 are offered voluntary positions in social service work involving children, the elderly or handicapped. The commitment is usually for at least a year.

Aufbauwerk der Jugend in Deutschland e.V.
Zur Kalk Laute 21, D-3550 Marburg.
Opportunities for young people aged 16 to 25 to take part in work camps held under canvas and on a self-catering basis. Knowledge of German may be required.

Christlicher Friendensdienst e.V. (CFD)
Rendelerstrasse 9-11, D-6000 Frankfurt-am-Main 60.
Peace-oriented work camps held both in Germany and other countries for applicants aged 18 or above.

IBO-Gemeinschaftsdienste Internationaler Bauordern Deutscher Zweig e.V.
Postfach 770, D-6520 Worms.
Work camps for youngsters aged 16 plus interested in working on building construction projects.

Internationaler Begegnung in Gemeinschaftsdiensten e.V. (IBG)
Schlosser Strasse 28, D-7000 Stuttgart 1.
Rural projects for applicants aged 18 to 30 interested in working on such things as forestry and farmwork.

Internationaler Jugendgemeinschaftsdienste e.V. (IJGD)
Kaiserstrasse 43, D-5400 Bonn 1
Applicants aged 18 to 25 with a basic knowledge of German can apply for places in about 100 work camps held in Germany each year including some in Berlin. With basic accommodation, meals and insurance included, the projects are designed to help a range of socially disadvantaged groups.

Nothelfergemeinschaft der Freund e.V. (NDF)
Auf der Körnerwiese 5, D-6000 Frankfurt-am-Main 1.
Open to youngsters aged from 16 years interested in community projects to assist the elderly and sick.

Service Civil International Deutscher Zweig e.V. (SCI)
Blücherstrasse 14, D-5300 Bonn 1.
Organises about 40 work camps each year based on ecological and cultural projects. Basic food and accommodation included.

Volksbund Deutsche Kriegsgräberfürsorge e.V.
Werner Hilpert Strasse 2, Postfach 103840, D-5300 Kassel.
Organisation which maintains German war graves. Provides short term (two to three weeks) work camp opportunities for young people aged 17 to 25.

Working with children or students
For young people, there are work opportunities through au pair arrangements, and the supervision of children/teenagers at camps of various kinds. Among the organisations to contact are:

AFS Interkulturelle Begegnungen e.V.
Warburgstrasse 35, Postfach 300342, D-2000 Hamburg 36.
Homstay and exchange programmes of various kinds for young people.

Aufbauwerke der Jugend, Gemeinschaft für den Freiwilligen Internationalen Arbeitseinsatz e.V.
Bahnhofstrasse 26, D-3550 Marburg.
Invites applications from young people aged 18 to 26 years, for their programme of international work camps.

Bund der Deutschen Katholischen Jugend (BDKJ)
Antonius Strasse 3, Postfach 1229, D-7314 Wernau.
Applicants aged 18 to 35 having some experience of looking after children are sought to work in the summer months, supervising groups of children and teenagers.

Katholische Mädchensozialarbeit
Karlstrasse 40, D-7800 Freiburg.
Can arrange au pair and other short term work opportunities, in some cases up to a whole year. Language courses are available along with board and lodging with German families. The association is part of the Association Catholique Internationale des Services de la Jeunesse.

Pädagogischer Austauschdienst im Sekretariat der Ständigen, Konferenz der Kultusminister der Länder in der Bundesrepublik Deutschland
Nassestrasse 8, D-5300 Bonn 1.
Opportunities for foreign language assistants to work a few hours a week helping local German teachers.

3
On Arrival

MONEY MATTERS

Currency
The monetary unit in Germany is the *Deutschemark* (DM), which is divided into one hundred *Pfennigs*.

Notes: DM 5, 10, 20, 50, 100, 500, 1000
Coins: Pfennigs 1, 2, 5 (rare nowadays), 10, 50; DM 1, 2, 5

Learning a new currency system takes time, so it is a good idea before you leave home to get a packet of German money through your bank. You and your family can practise and become comfortable with the notes and coins and their values, and you will have one less thing to adjust to when you first arrive. Having a supply of German coins and small notes will make tipping porters and paying taxis on arrival much less confusing. If you are unable to get German money prior to your departure, the flight attendant may be able to change a small amount.

A currency exchange office (*Geldwechsel* or *Wechselstube*) or a bank can be found at most airports and major railway stations. Currency exchange offices are numerous and are sometimes open past regular banking hours. You can, of course, exchange money at a hotel, but you will generally receive a lower rate of exchange.

Germany has no currency restrictions either incoming or outgoing.

Almost everything in Germany is expensive, especially housing. Shopping at the weekly markets is a good way to save on fruits, vegetables and flowers as well as to ensure that you are purchasing the freshest produce. In addition, look for local beers and wines, for which Germany is famous. Since Germany belongs to the European Community, there are no high import tariffs on goods from other member nations.

Banking and credit cards

Opening a German bank account is a wise move. One reason is convenience: it is not easy to get personal foreign cheques cashed in business places or hotels (although British Eurocheques can be used at major banks). Getting a local German cheque cashed, however, is quite easy. You can also have regular bills (such as rent, phone, etc) paid by bank transfer orders. You might want to investigate this system, particularly if you are out of the country frequently. German banks do not return cancelled cheques or provide monthly statements, so keeping accurate records is important.

Another alternative is opening a Postal Savings Account at the post office, where you can not only pay most bills for only a few Pfennigs but can also open a savings account. Enquire about this on arrival.

Credit cards are not widely accepted. Several international credit cards are accepted in hotels, airlines, major shops, and some restaurants, but in most places you will need cash.

Taxes

Individuals registered as permanent residents of Germany are taxed on all income and benefits from sources both inside and outside of Germany. However, under double taxation conventions, your income will not be fully taxed by both your home and the German governments. Those not permanently residing in the Federal Republic are subject only to limited income tax on the income acquired there. You should check your tax position before accepting an offer of employment. Your local Inspector of Taxes will be able to give you detailed guidance before you leave the UK.

Tax rates are steeply progressive and cover indirect as well as direct benefits (i.e. employer contributions to pension plans, etc.). Narrowly defined deductions are allowed for 'expenditures to create, protect or preserve income'. Foreigners may request a special 'lump sum deduction' called a *Pauschalierung.*

Cars are subject to a tax based on cylinder capacity; there are also minimal annual taxes on radios and television sets.

Value added tax (VAT) is levied on a wide range of goods and services, as in the UK.

Tax laws are complex; be sure to get good tax advice before you leave for Germany. If you need additional assistance when you are there, and your employer is unable to provide it, your embassy will usually help.

Tipping
Tipping is customary in the FRG and the following guidelines will generally apply:

- Hotels and restaurants: a 10-15 per cent service charge is added to your bill (in addition to the VAT).
- Porters: DM 2 per bag.
- Hotel maids: DM 2-5 per night.
- Taxi drivers: 10 per cent of the fare.
- Cloakroom attendants: small change.
- Hairdresser: 10-15 per cent of the total charge.
- Hotel concierge: for special services (amount depends on the service supplied).
- Cinema and theatre ushers: no tip expected.

In general, special services should be rewarded.

TIME AND DATES

Germany is one hour ahead of Greenwich Mean Time (GMT) during the winter, and one hour ahead of British Summer Time in the summer. Daylight Savings Time is in effect between late March and late September. The dates vary but are announced in advance in all local papers. As is true all over Europe, Germans use the international time system, with the twenty-four hour clock (8:00 pm is 2000; 9:30 pm is 2130).

Business hours
Most business offices are usually open from 0830 to 1700, but factories generally start earlier. As in most cities, the streets are filled with traffic by 0700.

Banking hours are from 0830 to 1230 or 1300 and from 1430 to 1600, Monday to Friday, except for Thursdays, when banks close at 1730.

Shops are open from 0800 or 0900 to about 1830 on weekdays; they close on Saturdays at 1400 except on the first Saturday of each month, when shops stay open until 1800 or 1830. In many outlying districts and rural villages, the 1300-1500 'siesta closing' is still practised.

Post offices (*Postämter*) are open from 0800 until noon and again from 1400 to 1730; they close at noon on Saturdays. (German public post-boxes are yellow.)

Government offices are usually open from 0830 to 1730 during the week and are closed on Saturdays.

Chemists (*Apotheken*) generally observe shop hours and will display a special sign if they are open all night and on Sundays.

Public holidays
Businesses normally close on the following public holidays:

1 January	New Year's Day
March/April (dates vary)	Good Friday and Easter Monday
1 May	Labour Day
May (date varies)	Ascension Day
May/June (varies)	Whit Monday
June (varies)	Corpus Christi Day (Catholic areas)
17 June	German Unity or Berlin Day
1 November	All Saints' Day (Catholic areas)
November (varies)	Repentance Day
25 December	Christmas Day
26 December	Second Day of Christmas

Business slows down between 1 June and 30 August (it seems all Europe is on holiday in August) as well as before and after the Christmas and Easter holidays.

Numbers
Numbers are written in a way that may be unfamiliar to you. A horizontal line is drawn through the leg of the number seven so that it looks a bit like a reversed *F* (7); this differentiates it from the one, which often looks quite like our seven (7). If you want

Mitzfahrzentralen
The new alternative to hitch-hiking

This is a convenient and inexpensive way of getting around the Republic if you want to avoid paying full commercial fares on the one hand, and are nervous about hitch-hiking on the other. The *mitzfahrzentralen* are agencies through which you can arrange lifts almost anywhere in Germany. You just telephone a few days before you plan to make your trip, and the agency will try and match you with someone making a similar journey. The costs of course depend on the distance, and it is even possible to bring together drivers and travellers who are for example both women, or non-smokers. You should check out the insurance cover.

Contacts
Aachen	Roermonder Strasse 4, D-5100 Aachen
Berlin	Kurfürstendamm 227, D-1000 Berlin 15
Bonn	Herwarthstrasse 11a, D-5300 Bonn 1
Bremen	Humboldtstrasse 6, D-2800 Bremen
Düsseldorf	Kölnerstrasse 212, D-4000 Düsseldorf 1
Freiburg	Belfortstrasse 55, D-7800 Freiburg
Hamburg	Högerdamm 26, D-2000 Hamburg 1
Heidelberg	Hauptstrasse 118, D-6900 Heidelberg
Köln	Saarstrasse 22, D-5000 Köln 1
München	Amalienstrasse 87, D-8000 München 40
Stuttgart	Lerchenstrasse 68, D-7000 Stuttgart 1
Wiesbaden	Rüdesheimer Strasse 29, D-6200 Wiesbaden
Würzburg	Am Zinkhof, D-8700 Würzburg

Many university towns also have Mitzfahrzentralen.

Guide books
Mitzfahrzentralen: Addressen & Tips für In- & Ausland, Verlag W. Richter, Wörthstrasse 24, D-8000 München 80.

Nix Wie Weg: Mitzfahrzentralen in Deutschland und Anderswo, Prolix Verlag, Postfach 6120, D-7200 Freiburg.

to indicate a number on your fingers, you should start counting from your thumb (thumb for one, thumb and index finger for two, etc.). The full point and comma are used differently as well. A full point separates billions, millions, thousands and hundreds; the comma only sets off the decimal fraction, for example, 100.290,55.

TRANSPORT

Transport is modern and very efficient in Germany. Railways and highways are excellent, and the network of navigable rivers and canals carries a great volume of freight (all railways, airports and seaports, and major bus lines are government owned). Rental cars are available and taxi services are good. Getting around should not be difficult.

Transport in cities
Taxis
Fares vary from city to city and are based on time, zones and distances. You will be charged an extra fee for each suitcase and, if it applies, for your dog. You can order cabs by phone for a small surcharge or pick them up at taxi stands. Although tipping is not compulsory, most people tip the driver about DM 1 or 2 for fares up to DM 10 and about 10 per cent for higher fares.

Trams, buses and underground trains
Public transport is clean, quick, efficient and plentiful and is a good way to see a new city as well as to get around efficiently and inexpensively. Purchase bus and tram tickets from the conductor or from a ticket dispenser, or sometimes from the driver. In the larger cities, you can purchase a booklet of tickets if you use the bus or tram regularly. The bus stop sign (*Bushaltestelle*) is easy to see; in some places you may see *Bedarfshaltestelle*, (stop on request). Unless someone is waiting at the stop and signals the bus driver, the bus will not stop.

Underground railways (*U-Bahn*) operate in Berlin, Hamburg, Frankfurt, München, Bonn and Düsseldorf, providing an excellent means of transport. Lines extend into the suburbs from the city centres, and the fare is the same, no matter how far you travel. If you use this service regularly, purchase a book of tickets which gives you a small saving over the individual fares. The underground does not run between 0100 and 0500.

Telephone dialling codes

Dialling to Germany

West (01049-)
Aachen **241**
Augsburg **821**
Berlin (West) **30**
Bielefeld **521**
Bochum **234**
Bonn **228**
Bottrop **2041**
Braunschweig **531**
Bremen **421**
Bremerhaven **471**
Cologne (Köln) **221**
Darmstadt **6151**
Dortmund **231**
Duisburg **203**
Düsseldorf **211**
Essen **201**
Frankfurt/Main **69**
Freiburg **761**
Gelsenkirchen **209**
Hagen **2331**
Hamburg **40**
Hannover **511**
Heidelberg **6221**
Herne **2323**
Karlsruhe **721**
Kassel **561**
Kiel **431**

Koblenz **261**
Krefeld **2151**
Leverkusen **214**
Lübeck **451**
Ludwigshafen/Rhein **621**
Mainz **6131**
Mannheim **621**
Mönchengladbach **2161**
M'gladbach-Rheydt **2166**
Mülheim/Ruhr **208**
Munich **89**
Münster **251**
Neuss **2101**
Nuremberg **911**
Oberhausen **208**
Offenbach/Main **69**
Oldenburg, Oldb **441**
Osnabrück **541**
Recklinghausen **2361**
Regensburg **941**
Remscheid **2190**
Saarbrücken **681**
Solingen **212**
Stuttgart **711**
Wiesbaden **6121**
Wilhelmshaven **4421**
Wuppertal **202**
Würzburg **931**

East (01037-)

Berlin (East) **2**
Cottbus **59**
Dressau **47**
Dresden **51**
Eisenach **623**
Erfurt **61**
Frankfurt/Oder **30**
Gera **70**
Halle (Saale) **46**
Jena **78**
Karl-Marx-Stadt **71**
Leipzig **41**
Magdeburg **91**
Plauen **75**
Potsdam **33**
Rostock **81**
Stralsund **821**
Suhl **66**
Torgau **407**
Zeitz **450**

Dialling from Germany

Country codes:
Australia **0061**
Great Britain **0044**
Ireland **00353**
United States **001**

On Arrival

Trains
One of the joys of travelling in Europe is using the trains, and the German railway system is among the best. Trains are fast, comfortable and reliable though not always frequent. Long-distance trains are especially pleasant. As a train leaves a station, the conductor will announce the next stop. Be ready to get off the trains the minute they stop, as they often stay in the stations only a brief time. Arrivals and departures are not normally announced inside the stations; one watches for the predicted time of arrival and for station signs. There are a number of different types of trains:

- *Personenzug*: local train, stops at all stations.
- *E-Zug*: stops often but not at every station.
- *D-Zug*: express train.
- *IC-Zug*: intercity express (sometimes carries multilingual secretaries as a service to businesspeople).
- *TEE*: Trans-European Express (first class only, reservation required).

Air service
Frankfurt is Germany's most active international airport and air transport hub. There are international facilities in most major cities as well, but flights will generally make a stop in Frankfurt. Additionally, there are frequent flights between the major cities. Lufthansa, the German national airline, is known for its fine service. Of course, all major international airlines service the Federal Republic (see chapter 11 for information on specific cities).

COMMUNICATIONS

The telephone system
Public phones, which are owned by the postal system, are bright yellow in colour and are not as numerous as you might expect. Because the system is fully automated, you cannot make any operator-assisted calls from these phones. To make a collect or credit-card call, you must use your own phone or go to the post office.

There are two types of phones in each booth: the *Telephon*

or *Ortsgespräche* for local calls only (no time limit), and the *Ferngespräche* for local and long-distance calls. You can dial any long-distance call within the republic by depositing several coins before dialling. Unused coins will be returned automatically at the end of your call.

Rates are reduced after 1800 and at weekends, with the lowest rate (night rate) applying between 2200 and 0600 daily and all day Saturday, Sunday and holidays.

Try to avoid charging long-distance calls on your hotel bill because the surcharges can be extremely high. For information on obtaining a phone call in your house/flat, see chapter 6.

The Yellow Pages (*Gelbe Seiten*) contain essentially the same type of information as they do elsewhere. On page 1 you find emergency numbers and listings for directory assistance, repair service, telegram service, time, weather, and other information services. Current postal rates are listed on page 3. Entries are arranged alphabetically and there is an index at the end of the book. If you find a 'Q' next to the phone number, that means the phone will be answered by a recording. Free copies are available at your post office if there is no copy in your house or flat.

The White Pages provide personal and business phone numbers and addresses arranged in alphabetical order. Area codes (*Vorwahlen*) are listed in a small yellow book that comes with the White Pages. These are generally posted above the phone in public phone booths as well.

Postal service

The postal service, like most of the transport system, is owned by the government and is excellent. Post is delivered once a day—in the morning. Stamps are available at post offices or hotels.

The Federal Republic (and West Berlin) has been divided into eight main postal districts. The biggest city in each district has a one-digit postal number (1 Berlin, 2 Hamburg, etc.) and towns within that district have 2, 3 or 4 numbers according to size. Frankfurt, for example, is 6; Wiesbaden, being smaller but in the Frankfurt postal district, is 62; Idstein, a smaller town near Wiesbaden and within its subdistrict, is 627; a little village outside Idstein is 6271.

The logic in addressing envelopes German-fashion is to proceed in order of importance—first the name of the addressee, on the next line the code number and name of the city or town, then the name of the street and the house number. Underline the town or city and put the code number to the left.

The post office handles telegrams, telephone and telex services, and collects radio and TV fees. It also offers a banking service, with both savings and cheque accounts, and a subscription service for newspapers and magazines. Cables can be sent from private phones or from the post office. It also pays out social security and other federal pensions and has a fleet of post buses which carry passengers.

Telex service is part of the postal system and is widely used in Germany; you can set up charge or credit arrangements. Telex service is also often available in hotels, at trade fairs, etc.

Radio and TV
Although Germany has nine radio stations, most local programming originates from either Hamburg or Köln, the two large regional stations. A wide variety of programmes, including extensive news coverage, is available. English-language programmes are also broadcast by the BBC, Radio Luxembourg, and the American Armed Forces in Germany. Radio Stuttgart carries many English-language broadcasts as well, including facts and information about Germany, the people and their lives. It also broadcasts practical information about the weather, road conditions and current activities. The American radio station 'RIAS' beams programmes to the Soviet Union from West Berlin. With proper equipment, you can pick up these broadcasts throughout Germany and in other European countries.

A shortwave radio is welcome because it helps you keep up with sports, music and news from home. It also gives you access to music from Moscow and La Scala or the great festivals of Salzburg or Edinburgh and permits some 'eavesdropping' on the Voice of America and Radio Free Europe.

There are two government-operated TV networks (called *Programmes* in Germany) and a third regional network which operates daily, broadcasting plays, opera, news, etc. A small monthly tax on both TV and radio sets provides the Programmes with operating funds and allows them greater independence since they don't have to rely on advertising (of which there is very little) for operating income. Although state-owned stations are independent, they are supervised by a non-government civil authority.

Publications

This highly literate nation has 1,250 daily newspapers and about 9,400 periodicals, all privately owned. *Das Bild*, published in Hamburg, is the largest and most influential German-language newspaper, with a circulation of nearly five million. *Der Spiegel*, also published in Hamburg, is the German equivalent of *Time* or *Newsweek*. The German Press Agency (DPA—*Deutsche Presse Agentur*) is the leading news service, with offices all over the world.

English-language publications

Major international papers and magazines are available one to three weeks after publication. British and French newspapers and the International Herald Tribune are available on a current daily basis. The European or international editions of *Time* and *Newsweek* are available on the date of issue. The larger bookshops carry limited selections of books in English, and some English-language paperbacks are available in train stations and airports as well. Unfortunately, though, books are very expensive.

The *German Tribune* is an English-language weekly that summarises major stories that have appeared in the German press; it can be ordered from the *German Tribune*, Friedrich Reinecke Verlag GmbH, D-2000 Hamburg 76, 23 Schöne Aussicht, Federal Republic of Germany.

Aussenpolitik, a quarterly foreign affairs review, is available in an English edition; the publisher will send a sample copy at no obligation. It can be ordered from Interpress GmbH, D-2000 Hamburg 76, Holsteinischer Kamp 14, Federal Republic of Germany.

LANGUAGE

To get the most out of your stay in Germany, try your hardest to learn German. While you will find that many Germans do speak English and that you can get along without learning German, you will greatly increase your enjoyment and understanding of Germany and the German people if you can speak the language. Even if your German is far from perfect, people will respect you and respond warmly to your efforts.

One of the most important German words for you to know and use is *bitte*. Bitte (bit' tah) is the word for both 'please' and 'you are welcome'. To acknowledge an apology, reply '*bitte schön*' or '*bitte sehr*', meaning essentially 'don't mention it'. When you hold a door open for someone, pick up something that has fallen, hand someone a forgotten paper—any small courtesy—accompany it with a smile, a nod and the word *bitte*. When you are offered seconds of food in a German home or restaurant, 'bitte,' or 'ja, bitte' (ya bit' tah) indicates acceptance.

If you want to say 'no, thank you', you may, depending on the context, simply use the word *danke* (dahng' kah), or *nein, danke* (nine' dahng kah).

There are two ways to say 'excuse me', each with a different meaning. If you step on or bump into someone and want to excuse yourself, you say *Verzeihung, wie bitte?* (fehr tsigh' ung vee bit' tah), 'forgive or pardon me please'. This same phrase also means 'I beg your pardon'. If, however, you want to ask if you may pass or get by someone, you say *gestatten sie* (ge shtah' ten zee) *bitte*, which means 'please permit me'. More commonly used is simply *pardon*, with the accent on the second syllable.

People tend to greet each other with some vigour, so a hearty *Guten Morgen* (goo' ten mor' gen)—or whatever greeting is appropriate for the time of day—should be used. When departing, a sincere *Auf Wiedersehen* (owf vee' der zey en) is appreciated.

Schools and institutes teaching German have multiplied in all major German cities. Consult the Yellow Pages of your local phone book. Embassies, consulates, churches and clubs can provide additional leads. You can also get a private tutor or a student to come to supper certain nights a week and help the family with the language. Another alternative is simply to put yourselves in German-speaking environments where you will have to listen and speak in German.

Another good way to pick up German is to go to the cinema to watch German films and to listen to German on radio and TV. Even if you do not understand what is being said, your ears are becoming accustomed to the language, and before long you will be able to pick out single words, then phrases, then the main idea of the programme. Children's television shows can also be a useful learning tool.

When you shop, pay attention to labels—read everything. It will help you add useful nouns and verbs to your vocabulary as well as make your shopping more efficient in the long run. Frequent the small local shops for your groceries and learn how to place your order in German. After a while you will be able to carry on a simple conversation with the shopkeepers. If you are a loyal customer, the shopkeepers will be quite willing to talk and put up with your broken German. Just don't be afraid to use your new vocabulary. You'll both be able to have a good laugh over your faux pas in German.

Children or older people in your neighbourhood can also be good helpers. Both groups always seem to have enough time to chat and are interested in sharing information with newcomers.

In short, use as many methods to learn German as you can, particularly those fitted to your particular style of learning. And use German as often as you can.

4
Values and Customs

Two words which underlie most German social customs are *reserve* and *formality*, and both are expressed in a number of ways. While the attitudes and behaviours discussed in this section will not be true for everyone, they will provide a broad framework within which some of the reactions of the Germans can be understood.

The following quotes indicate how many Germans would think of themselves in comparison with, for example, British or American visitors.

'You delight in being occupied. We believe in contemplation.'

'You say, "business before pleasure." We close our store and go on holiday.'

'You are accustomed to new programmes and schedules. Frequent change bothers us.'

'You sell your home and move into a new one. We are the third generation to live in ours.'

'You admire film stars and athletes. We admire professors.'

'You dye your hair and watch your weight to retain a youthful appearance. We let nature take its course.'

'You pursue happiness. We are content with good health.'

'You believe in sharing everything almost immediately: your thoughts, your feelings, your possessions. We are more careful in our choices of those whom we trust, whom we love and share things with.'

CONSCIENTIOUSNESS

A job well done is something to be proud of, and doing things well and thoroughly is very important to the conscientious German. The German housewife considers herself to be the best housekeeper in the world and resents being told how to do things more efficiently or more economically. She is slow to change and considers an idea a long time before adopting it. And doing a job well doesn't mean that it is done fast. Don't expect a twenty-four-hour rush job from the cleaners (or anyone). Careful thought and planning go into anything that is efficient, worthwhile and respectable. For a German there is no such thing as learning a trade or business by trial and error. One should learn it at school or in a training programme, no matter how long it takes. (This also applies to language learning!)

RESPECT FOR THE INTELLECTUAL

Intelligence is a German's most valuable asset, and gaining knowledge is not an individual endeavour; the state pays for education. Germans praise ideas rather than deeds and admire the well-educated intellectual who can think and reason, whether his or her ideas are implemented or not. Action is not as important as the idea behind it. A German's list of most admired persons would generally be headed by a professor, even though professors produce no marketable 'product'.

Intelligence is demonstrated in many ways: a broad education, social grace, speaking and spelling correctly. To be ignorant of something is degrading to a German—quite different from the common attitude that a lack of knowledge is all right as long as you admit to it.

Conversely, we may admire the kind of intelligence that can be used to create practical results or convert ideas into products. We like to see results and don't especially care if the person producing them has obtained an advanced education. In fact those who have succeeded without the benefit of formal study are frequently admired for their achievement.

PRIVACY

The German need for privacy manifests itself in numerous ways, some of which are also found elsewhere in northern Europe. Office doors, and doors in general, are usually closed in Germany. Fences and large gates surround dwellings throughout Europe. The need for privacy has its roots in Europe's violent history and also in the sheer density of population. Europeans are not accustomed to wide open spaces. Because of these historical influences, European tradition leans towards mistrusting a stranger rather than welcoming him or her and towards clearly defining personal space rather than allowing the boundaries to be ambiguous.

FORMALITY

The German may strike you as being cold and formal, but you should not interpret this formality as avoidance. It is rather an expression of respect. Often in our society, the better you know someone, the more casual you can be with that person. The German feels that bonds should be built on respect rather than on casualness.

Social prestige is determined in large measure by profession. While wealth, family history and land ownership play a role in conferring status, education and individual achievement are perceived as the key to social standing. Thus, titles earned from intellectual effort are important. Germans address each other (with only few exceptions) using *Herr, Frau* or *Fraulein*, followed by either title, family name, or both, for example: Herr *Doktor* Schmidt (for both medical and academic doctors) or Herr *Professor*, with or without a name. You may hear people addressed with multiple honorifics ('Herr Professor *Advocat*') as a further acknowledgement of multiple degrees or professions. A useful term which fits the head of any business, government office, hotel, or the like is *Direktor*. If you do not know someone's name but do know his or her occupation, you can feel comfortable using the title only, for example, Herr or Frau Doktor or Herr/Frau Direktor. First names are usually used only by family members or very close acquaintances or friends. Do not address someone by his or her first name unless asked to do so.

Gnädige Frau is the most polite form of address; it conveys respect and is appropriate when greeting older or high-ranking women. If you don't know someone's name, you can simply address a woman as Frau and a man as Herr. A woman may be addressed by her own first name (not her husband's, eg Frau Gerda Maier, not Frau Hans Maier). When addressing envelopes, use Herr or

Frau plus the title and name, for example, Frau Dr (usually abbreviated) Gerda Maier or Frau Gerda Maier. When addressing an envelope to both husband and wife, use Herr Hans Maier and Frau.

Young Germans are less title-conscious than the older generation, as are those who have mixed a great deal with people from other countries. Young people use *Du* (informal 'you') easily with their peers; this informality is also common among manual labourers. Office colleagues, however, normally use *Sie* (the formal, polite 'you'), as do people you meet in most other situations. As with first names, do not use Du unless asked to do so. These language rules don't apply when using English, of course, but other ways of expressing informality and familiarity should be avoided until the relationship has developed to a point where a closeness and greater familiarity are appropriate. As in almost everything, let the host be the leader.

HANDSHAKING

The German form of greeting is the handshake, not a smile. Smiles are a sign of friendship. (People aren't being unfriendly when they don't smile. They don't know you, so how can they feel a connection with you?) People in Europe, and especially Germans, shake hands constantly in both formal and informal situations, with friends as well as with acquaintances or strangers. If you stop to chat with someone on the street, you shake hands on meeting and on bidding farewell. When you enter the office and again before you leave at night, you shake hands with all your close colleagues. At small social gatherings, you shake hands with everyone on arrival (while stating your last name) and again on departure. At large parties, shaking hands with those to whom you are introduced is appropriate.

Following this ritual is often difficult for newcomers (especially the departing handshake, which is readily forgotten), but the impression you give (or do not give) makes this social convention well worth practising until you can do it without thinking or feeling self-conscious. The German handshake is firm, but not hard, and more of a 'clasping' than a 'pumping' gesture. And also worthy of note, the woman offers her hand for shaking before the man.

The German 'hand kiss' occurs in the air slightly above the hand. It is given only to married women or ladies of great esteem, and never outdoors. This is a practice not recommended to foreign men because it is a delicate, culturally rooted custom with which many foreigners are neither familiar nor comfortable. Women should not be startled, however, when German men make the gesture.

MANNERS

To British people, good manners are an indication of a good upbringing. To Germans good manners are a necessity for everyone, regardless of background or education. Germans realise that you are a foreigner and do not expect you to know about their customs, but poor manners will get you off to a bad start, which will be difficult if not impossible to compensate for at a later time. Good manners will be recognised and appreciated, so a bit of time spent in practising will be a valuable investment.

Children are taught from an early age how to behave and are expected to exhibit proper manners at all times. Boys are expected to make a slight bow when greeting an adult, and all children are taught to greet adults with a handshake and a good, strong greeting: 'Guten Morgen, Herr Schmidt', looking them straight in the eye. Teaching your children these small courtesies will go far in ensuring that they are accepted.

On the theory that the escort goes ahead to make sure everything is all right, men precede women through doors and into public places such as restaurants and theatres (and down theatre aisles). Since this is the opposite of the 'ladies first' custom, it may seem odd to us and warrants mention.

As a basic rule, a man walks on the left side of a woman in Germany, in the streets and elsewhere. The right side is the 'place of honour', so to speak. (Therefore, a young girl will always walk on the left side of an older woman.) The custom behind this is very old, originating in the Middle Ages when the gentleman would walk on the left so that he could draw his sword quickly and easily for the protection of his companion. However, when you are walking along a very narrow street, through heavy traffic, or along a dirty gutter, then the man walks on the side of the traffic (danger).

Men may or may not take a woman's arm when escorting her. Women shouldn't be surprised if a German woman acquaintance links arms with them while they are walking along the street. It is quite proper, quite common, and once you get used to it, quite a pleasant custom as well as a sign of friendship.

TIME: PROMPTNESS

Right on time, neither too early nor too late—that's the German attitude towards time. Being prompt when arriving at any appointment (business or social) is very important. If you are more than ten minutes late, a very good excuse is expected, along with apologies. To be as much as thirty minutes late is simply unacceptable, so if you are unavoidably detained, it is best to call as soon as possible and explain. When the time for an official or academic function is listed with the abbreviation 'c.t.' (*con tempore*), it will begin promptly at fifteen minutes after the hour. If 's.t.' (*sine tempore*) is given, the function begins on the hour.

Although punctuality is paramount, the Germans don't live the fast pace of life that is often associated with time consciousness. They prefer a slower lifestyle and do not think, as we may do, that 'time is money'.

FRIENDSHIP

The Germans make a clear distinction between *ein Freund* (a friend) and *ein Bekannte* (an acquaintance). One may have a close acquaintance for many years and still not consider the person to be ein Freund. Even the use of the Du form doesn't necessarily indicate that one is a friend. Ein Freund indicates a person with whom you spend a lot of time, with whom you share interests, and whom you would expect to help in an emergency. In other words, a friend is someone to whom you would give 'the shirt off your back'—and more.

The words *Du* and *Freund*, then, are only used to indicate very special relationships, more like a 'close or best friend' in our society. It takes a long time for a friendship to develop because it requires that a lot of attention, interest and even financial assistance (if needed) be given to the other person. Since Germans do not move from place to place very much, friends are generally close geographically as well as emotionally. Because of the strong commitment involved, it is understandable that people are cautious about becoming involved. Once this lifetime commitment is made, the ensuing relationship is very close, extremely rewarding, highly valued, and potentially demanding.

SOCIAL CUSTOMS

Invitations

If you say to a German, even a casual acquaintance, that you would 'like to get together some day', you will be taken literally. Your acquaintance will expect a specific invitation, and if it is not forthcoming, the omission will be considered poor manners on your part.

If you must refuse an invitation, any reasonable excuse is acceptable. Only sickness and official business are valid excuses when cancelling an engagement, however, and the hosts should be notified as soon as possible.

When you are invited to someone's home for the first time, it is customary to take some flowers or chocolates to the hostess. If you should forget, it is acceptable to send them afterwards with a thank-you note. A florist can suggest the appropriate flowers. You should purchase an odd number of flowers (3, 5, 7, etc) to indicate that you don't want this visit to be the last one. Since red roses mean love, they do not make a good hostess gift under ordinary circumstances. Chrysanthemums should also be avoided as they are associated with funerals. Before giving the flowers to your hostess, you should remove all wrapping except cellophane from around them.

If a party is likely to be large, or if it is being given in your honour, send flowers in advance with a note stating how much you are looking forward to the evening.

The host and hostess usually greet guests at the door, shake hands, and help them with their coats (see information on handshaking above). When two couples greet each other, the women shake hands first. When a German guest arrives at your home for any event, no matter how simple, he or she will almost invariably say 'thank you for your invitation'. It is courteous for you to do the same when arriving at a German home.

Strangers do not introduce themselves if the hostess is busy; they wait to be introduced. Women do not stand when being introduced unless it is someone much older than themselves or someone of high rank.

Europeans feel that strong alcohol (spirits) and smoking both dull the taste buds and prevent the enjoyment of fine food, so there is no smoking during a meal, and the cocktail hour before a meal is short (all the more reason to be prompt). Wine and beer are served during the meal, and cigarettes (perhaps with brandy) may be offered after coffee.

All in all, German hosts tend to be very gracious; they expend every effort to make their guests welcome and to ensure an enjoyable evening. There are so few rules that it should not be difficult to relax and enjoy social occasions. Just remember to shake hands.

'Setting a good table' is important to personal pride but is also a sign of hospitality. An invitation for *Abendbrot* (literally 'evening bread') indicates the meal will be an informal one while *Abendessen* (evening meal) indicates a more formal dinner.

Thank-you notes, preferably handwritten, are expected after any kind of dinner or party in someone's home—unless you know your host and hostess extremely well.

Toasts

It is not good manners to drink at a party before the host. He will raise his wine glass to the lady on his right, then toast the health of the group. You should do the same when you are host. The most usual phrase is *zum Wohl* (to your health), but the host or hostess usually adds a few words of greeting or good wishes.

After this initial courtesy, people drink as they wish. Often there are toasts among guests initiated by the person of higher rank, with the lower-ranking guest returning the toast a little later in the evening. At the time, the toast is acknowledged with a smile and a little nod of the head. Between men and women, it is always the man who makes the overture first.

The clinking of glasses usually occurs only at some special event like New Year's Eve or a birthday, and only glasses with wine or champagne are clinked together—never beer, brandy or spirits. Hold a wine glass by its stem. Except when you are drinking brandy, it is considered bad form to hold a glass by its body, for this heats the wine too much.

Informal visits

Germans are not accustomed to 'dropping in' on one another. Among close friends and relatives, informal visits may occur during the Sunday coffee hour, but acquaintances and newcomers should phone before visiting. Phone calls during mealtime (between one and three o'clock and between six and eight) should be avoided. When possible, Germans prefer to eat their heavy meal in the middle of the day, but this is becoming increasingly difficult to accomplish because of modern work schedules and traffic.

Germans are generally rather reserved and prefer to allow others, especially foreigners, to make the first move. Inviting neighbours for coffee and dessert (or perhaps a glass of wine) on a weekend afternoon may lead to friendly relations, but you will probably have to take the initiative. The *Kaffeeklatsch* usually takes place in the afternoon—often the only time women can gather with their friends for 'a coffee' at the café.

CONVERSATION AND PERSONAL STYLE

It is easy to be poised when being introduced; all you need to do is shake hands and say *Guten Tag* (or *Guten Morgen* or *Guten Abend*), Frau (Herr) . . . You don't have to go on with *Wie geht es lhnen* (How are you?) or any other phrase. *Wie geht es lhnen* is intended as an enquiry about the well-being of someone you already know, and the answer may be quite detailed. (In fact, its use with a stranger or new acquaintance should be avoided; it is taken literally and therefore is quite personal and may offend.)

The best opening into anyone's language is genuine appreciation for the things of which the speakers of that language are proud. Too often we are not aware of these in another country and end up talking about ourselves. Try to open most conversations, particularly when you first arrive, with some complimentary and interested comment about the country, the city, sports, music, or whatever—not with a personal remark or question. Germans have a tremendous and justifiable pride in their extraordinary postwar economic growth, their historic towns and ancient architecture, and their famous musicians and artists. Spend some time learning about Germany's heroes, sources of pride and accomplishments so that you can talk about them easily. You will find this contributes considerably to your conversation skills, for your companion will almost surely expand on any subject you mention with pleasure and you will be off to a good start.

Germans are private people and resent being asked personal questions by people they have just met. Many of the questions which Germans may consider too personal are the very ones considered appropriate by us as ice breakers—questions about occupation or spouse and family. Also to be avoided are questions concerning finances, educational background, religious affiliation, and the Holocaust. The Second World War can be discussed in the context of personal experiences. This situation changes when you get to know someone well, of course. Let your German friend take the lead in discussing sensitive topics.

When you get to know Germans well, you will find that they tend to be direct, even blunt, in conversation, unlike many British people, who, though they admire honesty, consider it more tactful to leave some things unsaid. The ability to impart knowledge is, to the German, an important skill to which politeness may occasionally take a back seat.

The German does not consider it impolite to comment on unusual dress or to point out misbehaviour. Because they are concerned with honesty, they don't compliment often. A compliment is given only when a person has done something outstandingly well. If you give compliments too frequently, the German will be embarrassed or question your sincerity.

NIGHT LIFE

Germans enjoy a lively night life, which often includes dancing. It is customary for women to dance with any male who asks them. Brush up on your waltzes and polkas. Although young people follow the latest dance fads and rock groups, the older generation keeps much more to the more traditional styles of dancing.

Small local restaurants (similar to British pubs) abound and are called *Kniepen*. Many a pleasant evening can be spent in them eating, drinking, and just getting together.

If you go to a restaurant and find it crowded, don't be surprised if you are seated with strangers. The practice of sharing a table is quite common. It is sometimes difficult to get a glass of water in a restaurant. Germans, like most Europeans, are not accustomed to drinking water, and your waiter may ask you if you would like mineral water instead. Milk is also not commonly served; if you request it, you run the risk of being served warm milk.

SUMMARY

Traditions are very important to Germans because they are manifestations of their culture and thus give a sense of security. We may often adopt a trial-and-error approach to new ideas,

Values and Customs

whereas the Germans want to investigate to see if the new is better than the old before changing.

The following list summarises some of the points discussed in this or other chapters and suggests appropriate behaviour to use while you are learning more about German culture and behaviour. Gaining an understanding of the cultural assumptions and values that are fundamental to German patterns of behaviour is very important. The best way to learn is to observe and to ask for information when you do not understand or when you feel you may have done or said something inappropriate.

1. Shake hands the first time you see a colleague or acquaintance that day (except on the street, unless you want to stop and talk), both on meeting and on bidding farewell.

2. Teach your children to be polite when meeting Germans. They should shake hands and use a polite greeting, for example, *'Guten Tag, Herr Schmidt.'* At the beginning, a polite 'how do you do' or 'good morning' (afternoon, evening) is acceptable.

3. Use a person's title when addressing him or her: *Herr/Frau/Doktor* . . . If the person has more than one title, use the higher-ranking one, so you would address *Professor Doktor Mueller* as *Professor Mueller* (even though you may hear others using multiple honorifics).

4. If you don't know a person's name, you may address him or her by title only (*Doktor, Professor, Direktor*).

5. Don't address a German woman with her husband's first name (eg *Frau Hans Schmidt*); it is not customary.

6. Address all adult men with *Herr* and adult women with *Frau*, whether they are married or not.

7. Only use first names and *Du* when you have become very good friends. Let your German acquaintance take the lead in making the switch.

8. Friendship involves considerable commitment and attention but is very rewarding. Don't be discouraged if it takes a while.

9. Always be polite and use good manners; a bad first impression is difficult to change.

10. Take flowers for your hostess when you are invited to someone's house.

11. Do not drink until your host has drunk at the table. The proper toast is *Zum Wohl!* or *Prosit!* Glasses are clinked on special occasions and only when drinking wine or champagne.

12. Expect to be served coffee only after a meal (German coffee is normally fairly strong).

13. Remember to write a thank-you note after a dinner or party in someone's home.

14. Be prepared for a surprised look if you order milk or water in a restaurant; they are not commonly served.

15. Don't be surprised if strangers ask to sit down at your table in a restaurant, especially if the restaurant is crowded; this is quite the customary. You are not expected to converse with the other people beyond *Guten Tag* and *Auf Wiedersehen*.

16. At New Year, tip people who have been of service during the year, for example, the postman, newspaper boy, cleaning lady, etc.

17. When staying in a hotel, tip the concierge if he or she has helped you with some special service. Usually the concierge is the best source of information on sight-seeing, transport, or theatre tickets.

18. Don't rush a German. Remember, a job done well is more important than a job done quickly.

19. Be patient with red tape—there is a lot of it. Germany is a very regulated society.

20. Learn the language and have patience.

In general, don't expect Germans to be the same as British people—they are products of different cultures and traditions.

5
Doing Business in Germany

LANGUAGE

Although a working knowledge of English is increasingly common among younger people, only an estimated 20 per cent of older Germans speak English. If you use German, people will appreciate your effort, no matter how minimal your language skill or how imperfect your accent or pronunciation. Anything written in English should be accompanied by a German translation when presented in meetings or negotiations. Plan on taking an interpreter with you to any important conference. The burden is on you, the foreigner, to make sure you can communicate in an understandable manner. Translation services are readily available in the major cities, and major banks, trade fair administrations, or conference and convention centres can generally provide an interpreter. Another source of information and service is the Association of Translators and Interpreters: BDU (*Bundesverband der Dolmetscher und Ubersetzer* e.V.), 4100 Duisburg, Mulheimerstrasse; Tel: 357-480. Interpreters should be briefed before a meeting, especially if discussions are to be technical. In this case the interpreter should be provided, in advance, with a list of terms or technical words in order to become familiar with them before being required to translate them.

If you have drawings or specifications, they should be in German and in metric. This preparation not only saves time but gives a far better impression. Be generous with business cards, advertising materials (in German), and samples. These all help to increase your chances of being directed to the correct department and seeing the most appropriate person.

STYLE

Get to the point politely but quickly and know your subject well. The Germans are a thorough people who do not like their time wasted. The sort of preliminary courtesies and flourishes that are required among Spanish, French or Italians are wasted on Germans. After greetings and introductions (and a few brief comments on the weather or the most recent soccer match), they are anxious to get on with the job at hand; they do not like to chat before doing business. Formality is important as well, so avoid a breezy approach. Many people you meet will seem quite reserved, and it may take time to develop personal contacts, especially among those who have had little previous experience with foreign firms. (The younger your counterparts are, the friendlier and more informal they will be, as is true in other situations.) But, reserved or not, most businesspeople will offer liquid refreshment to office visitors (coffee, alcoholic beverages, or both). You should be prepared to do the same in your office.

Germans are working hard to hold their own domestic markets, which are under heavy competition from Japan and other Common Market countries. They give close and critical scrutiny to all new ideas and will look hard at both quality and price. Be prepared; make concrete, precise offers; confirm all agreements in writing. Approaches should be carefully planned. 'Playing it by ear' is not appreciated and won't get you far. Breaking an appointment or arriving even a few minutes late is a quick way to give a bad impression. A German may be so insulted by your poor manners that he or she will fail to hear your proposal, no matter how good it is. Germans are tough, good negotiators; they have a reputation for keeping their bargains, and they expect others to do the same.

Northern Germans are more reserved and efficient than southern Germans, whose lifestyle is much more relaxed. Whether you are in the north or the south, however, start all first meetings with considerable formality and continue in this manner until your German host or counterpart suggests otherwise. Use titles and last names when addressing your colleagues, and be particularly careful to avoid addressing secretaries by their first names. One needs to remember to shake hands on all occasions and to show respect for those of greater age or rank by such small courtesies as opening doors, helping with coats, or standing when they enter a room. Keep your jacket on and your tie pulled tight; avoid putting your feet on desks, chairs or train seats; sit up at your desk instead of leaning back with your hands behind your head. These are small things, but they give an impression of sloppiness in a country where proper behaviour is important.

Most northern Europeans, and definitely the Germans, value privacy and tend to close their office doors. This reflects a deep psychological difference from, for example, Americans, who feel an open door is friendly and a closed one is aloof. The closed door is a manifestation of the German's need for order and privacy, rather than an indication of aloofness. It also helps to keep the office or room warm, and in a country where heating costs are high, this is important. There is yet another reason for the closed door: it serves as an indicator to employees that they can work without the boss leaning over their shoulders.

It is hard to meet the top people in big German corporations and impossible without an appointment made well ahead of time. German directors delegate a great deal to lesser executives, and do little that does not directly concern their own job assignments.

Managers who sign *p.p.a.* before their names have the authority to negotiate for the organisation's management. This stands for *Prokurist*, meaning 'manager with registered signing authority'. An executive who signs *i.v.* with his or her name has the power to negotiate in some special areas for the firm. It means *in Vollmacht*, 'with authority'.

An important point to remember is that under both German and Swiss law, if you induce a party to believe a contract will be concluded and the contract does not materialise, you may be liable for damages. Be careful in this area, especially if your command of German is shaky.

BUSINESS ENTERTAINING

If you are invited to a restaurant, do not try to pay the bill. In general, the person who does the inviting for a business lunch or dinner picks up the tab. Lunch engagements should be made for around 1300 (most do not like to eat earlier) and supper appointments for about 1830. Business lunches usually last about an hour or an hour and a half. Dinner invitations are normally for 2000 and generally include spouses. Since German businesspeople try to keep private and business relations separate, an invitation to a home is quite an honour. Read the section 'Social Customs' in chapter 4 for dining etiquette.

It is not considered appropriate to discuss business outside the office. A business lunch may include some business talk, but even then the conversation will tend to be more general. Outside office hours—over golf or dinner, for example—avoid discussing business entirely.

SERVICES AVAILABLE TO UK BUSINESSES IN GERMANY

British Overseas Trade Board (BOTB)
The Focus German Team of the Exports to Europe Branch of the BOTB can offer advice on all aspects of exporting to Germany. (Focus Germany Team, BOTB, Room 374, 1 Victoria Street, London SW1H 0LT.)

Regional Offices of the BOTB are able to give information and guidance on general export matters.

Export Credits Guarantee Department
This government department provides UK suppliers of goods and services with insurance against the major financial risks of exporting and may enable such policy holders to obtain export finance. (Export House, 50 Ludgate Hill, London EC4M 7AY.)

Simplification of International Trade Procedures Board (SITPRO)
This is an independent organisation set up by the BOTB with the aim of simplifying export/import trade procedures and publishing information about the simplified systems to help British exporters to reduce costs and provide better service to customers. (Almack House, 26 King Street, London SW1W 6QW.)

German Chamber of Industry and Commerce in the UK
The aim of the Chamber is to promote trade and investment between the UK and the Federal Republic, in both directions. Membership now stands at 1200. Advice and information is available to non-members as well, though a charge may be made. (12/13 Suffolk Street, St James's, London SW1Y 4QH.)

British Commercial Representatives in Germany

These are the offices of the official British Commercial Representatives in Germany. Business visitors should write or telephone for appointments.

Berlin
Consul General
British Consulate-General
Uhlandstrasse 7-8
D-1000 Berlin 12
Tel: (030) 309 5295/7
Telex: 1894268 a/b
　UKBLIN D

Bonn
Counsellor (Commercial)
Commercial Department
British Embassy
Friedrich Ebert Allee 77
D-5300 Bonn 1
Tel: (0228) 23 40 61
Telex: 886887 a/b BRINF D
Fax: (01049) 228234070

Düsseldorf
Consul General
British Consulate-General
Nordsternhaus
Georg-Glock-Strasse 14
D-4000 Düsseldorf 30
Tel: (0211) 43740
Telex: 8-584855 a/b BRIN D
Fax: (01049) 2214542319

Frankfurt
Consul General
British Consulate-General
Bockenheimer Landstrasse 51-53
D-6000 Frankfurt am Main
Tel: (069) 720406/9
Telex: 414932
Fax: (01049) 69729553

Hamburg
Consul General
British Consulate-General
Harvestehuderweg 8a
D-2000 Hamburg 13
Tel: (04044) 60 71
Telex: 231562 a/b BRHBG
Fax: (01049) 404107259

Munich
Consul General
British Consulate-General
Amalienstrasse 62
D-8000 Munich 40
Tel: (08939) 40 15/9
Telex: 529959 a/b UKMUN D
Fax: (01049) 89331848

Stuttgart
British Marketing Office
　(Advanced Technology)
Kronprinzstrasse 14
D-7000 Stuttgart 1
Tel: (0711) 293216
Telex: 722397 a/b UKST D
Fax: (0711) 228271

British Chamber of Commerce in Germany

The British Chamber of Commerce in Germany exists to further British business interests in, and trade with, the Federal Republic. Membership now totals 650 companies, mostly agents or subsidiaries of UK exporters. Designed to supplement the work of the British Embassy and Consulates-General, the services of the Chamber are also available to non-member firms, although a fee may be charged for certain services. The wide range of publications includes information leaflets on, for example, German schools, employment law, salary surveys, etc. (D.5000 Köln 1, Heumarkt 14, Federal Republic of Germany. Tel: 0221-234284)

HIERARCHY IN GERMAN COMPANIES

Aktiengesellschaft (AG) employing more than five hundred people:

1. *Aufsichtsrat*—non-executive supervisory or advisory board elected by (a) the shareholders or their representatives and (b) the employees (codetermination). Members of the board of management may not be members of the supervisory board. The supervisory board appoints and supervises the *Vorstand*.

2. *Vorstand*—board of management, or executive board.
   Vorsitzer (also *Vorsitzender*)—chairman, president.
   Stellvertretender Vorsitz des Vorstandes—deputy chairman of the board.
   Ordentliches Mitglied des Vorstandes—regular member of the board.
   Stellvertretendes Mitglied des Vorstandes—deputy member of the board.

3. *Generalbevollmächtigter*—general manager.
   Abteilungsleiter—division/department head.
   Prokurist—corporate secretary.

SUMMARY SUGGESTIONS

The following suggestions summarise German business customs. It is important to become familiar with business practices in Germany, and some resources to help you are listed in the section on Further Reading at the end of this book.

The British Chamber of Commerce in Germany

Established in 1960, the BCCG has more than 600 member companies, and is a leading source of information, help and advice for firms and individuals trading or wishing to trade in Germany.

Summary of services
- Financial, commercial and statistical information, library
- Large range of contacts in most sectors
- Help with publicity and promotion including direct mail
- Opportunity to advertise in the BCCG yearbook
- Office services including message-taking, use of office equipment, secretarial back-up
- Consultancy services
- Official representation to German authorities

Some services are free to both members and non-members, though fees may be payable for other services. An important aspect of the work of the Chamber is in facilitating meetings and personal contacts, seminars, business lunches, discussion sessions and the like.

Summary of publications available from the Chamber

Industrial Property Rights in Germany
German Rules of Competition
German Control of Mergers and Acquisitions
How to Prepare for a German Tax Audit
German Labour Law
British Subsidiaries in Germany
British Investment in Germany
Setting up a Business in Germany Series:
  Choice of Legal Form
  Tax Aspects of an Investment
  Banking in Germany
  Premises
  The Employment of Staff
  Parent-Subsidiary Relationships
  Social Insurance and Employee Benefits
  Personal Taxation
  Living in Germany
Pursuance of Financial Claims in Germany
Legal Fees in Germany
Schooling in Germany
Determination of Income of Multinational Enterprises
Security for Bankers Advances
Discovery and Litigation
Acquisition of Private Companies
Germany Survey Reports:
  Salaries, Fringe Benefits and Conditions of Service
  Sales Performance of British Goods and Services
  British Subsidiaries: Productivity, Labour Relations and Profits
  Commercial use of English in Germany

British Chamber of Commerce in Germany, Heumarkt 14, D-5000 Köln 1. Tel: (0221) 234 284. Telex: (08) 883 400.

Doing Business in Germany

1. Always be on time for appointments; even a few minutes make a difference.

2. Be direct in all your business dealings; get to the point quickly and stay there.

3. Use direct eye contact and a formal approach; avoid breezy sales pitches.

4. Your body language should also reflect formality (no loose ties, shoes on desks, slouched posture).

5. Never sell a method or product on the merit that it is British—what works for the British does not necessarily work for Germans.

6. Don't assume your colleagues can speak English.

7. Anything written in English should be translated into German for meetings.

8. Find your own interpreter; don't expect your German counterpart to find one for you.

9. Convert relevant measurements to metric before making a presentation or submitting a report.

10. Remember to shake hands with all your associates the first time you see them each day and again upon departure in the evening.

11. Always call all your employees, including secretaries, by their title and last names; it is a sign of respect.

12. Offer liquid refreshment (coffee or alcoholic beverages) to office guests.

13. The person who does the inviting for a business lunch pays the bill. Although gratuity is included, special service warrants an additional tip.

14. Do not mix business with social occasions. Even business lunches tend to be social in nature.

15. Make concrete offers and be definite; your proposal will be carefully scrutinised.

6
Household Pointers

HOUSING

Although housing is in short supply all over Europe, the situation is critical in Germany. Modern, well-designed satellite towns have been and are being built near many of the cities, partly to supply new housing and partly to eliminate city slums. Unfortunately, this construction has supplied nowhere near the amount of housing needed.

Your housing search is likely to be slow and tedious, so be prepared for a lengthy stay at a hotel. In addition to hotels, be sure to enquire about pensions; 'holiday villages' are another possibility, especially if you have children (enquire at the local tourist office). Whatever your temporary quarters, you will want to be sure to carry (not ship) books, children's games, hobbies, language materials, and whatever else you think you will need during the first few weeks.

When you are looking for housing, keep in mind that location is more important than the number of rooms you have or the size of refrigerator that will fit. Experienced sojourners in Germany recommend that you conduct your house hunting with one eye on the underground, bus, or tram system. If you have children, being located near the school, or in an area with access to transport to the school, will be especially helpful.

There are several ways of going about your housing search. Estate agencies are one option. Although German estate agents are available, you may be able to find British agencies through the chamber of commerce, your consulate or bank. Many English-speaking expatriates have found these to be more helpful. Another possibility is the housing office (*Wohnungsamt*) of your city, which usually maintains a list of flats. The Municipal Tourist Office

(*Verkehrsamt*), a kind of cross between a chamber of commerce and tourist office, can provide you with a list of flats, houses or pensions where you can stay while searching for permanent housing and can sometimes provide long-term housing information.

Renting

Rent control ended in 1969; consequently, rents are high, and the estate agent's fee may be as much as two months' rent. Rents are based on square metres and, in general, are comparable to those in London.

When reading newspaper ads, there are several important words to watch for.

Leere Wohnung (unfurnished apartment) means exactly what it says, often even down to the towel rails, light fittings and mirrors. Built-in cupboards are rare; more often wardrobes are used and are supplied by the tenant.

Möblierte Wohnung (furnished apartment).

Möblierte Zimmer (furnished room).

Komfort indicates medium price, central heating and good plumbing.

Luxus indicates quality decor and fittings, more luxury.

Einfach means 'plain' and could even indicate that the kitchen and bath are shared.

Kaltmiete means that the heating is not included in the rent.

Some other terms and abbreviations you may see in the estate agent's details include the following:

NB	*Neubau* (new construction)
Erstbezug	First occupancy
Provision	Agent's fee, usually two months' rent
NK	*Nebenkosten* (utilities)
Kaution	Deposit against damage
Auflösung	Take-over fee, usually asked by previous tenant for furnishings

VB   *Vereinbarung* (price negotiable)
DHH   *Doppelhaushalt* (duplex)
REH or *RHM*   Terraced house, corner; terraced house, middle

Leases
Normally leases are written for two years, with a three-month notice for either party. The landlord cannot put you out without cause and even with cause must go to court to do so.

Be sure that you understand every word in the lease. A common clause, *Schönheitsreparaturen*, translates as 'beauty repairs' but really implies that the tenant must completely renovate the property when leaving. This used to be taken for granted but is no longer justified, given the high rents and short-term leases.

At the time you sign the lease, you will be asked to pay a three-month advance called 'caution money'. Like a security deposit, this money is kept as a guarantee that the tenant will pay for all necessary repairs accrued during tenancy. You should make sure that money is deposited in an interest-bearing account for you, not the landlord. In addition, to protect yourself from having to pay repairs for problems that existed before you moved in, make a careful inventory of all cracks, signs of wear in plumbing, peeling paint, holes, etc., and have your landlord initial the inventory before you sign the lease. Otherwise, most or all of your caution money will be eaten up with costly repairs instead of being returned to you. In short, be extremely thorough in protecting yourself. If you leave before the lease expires, you must sublet the apartment or house, forfeit the caution money, or pay the rent until the landlord finds a new tenant.

In many parts of Germany you, the occupant, are responsible for assisting in the maintenance of the grounds, basement, halls and pathways of a block of flats. You may also be responsible for repairs that are necessary while you live in the rented house or flat. The law requires that the occupant of a house with a chimney hire a chimney sweep to clean the chimney every two or three months.

House rules (*Hausordnungen*)
Be sure to enquire about the house rules, regulations which apply to both flats and houses and which may be unfamiliar. Some common rules include the following:

1. no baths late or early;

2. restrictions on when and how loudly you can play your radio/stereo/TV;
3. requirements such as locking an outside door after 2000 (difficult when you give a party).

Ask about the hours and extent to which children may play in the garden, etc. It should now be fairly obvious that renting is an ordeal—expensive and fraught with risk and unexpected expenses. The best advice is to proceed with caution and find someone knowledgeable and experienced to help you.

Home purchase

Although housing costs are high and estate agents' commissions may be as much as 5 per cent of the purchase price, you may decide it is financially advisable to purchase a home or flat, even for a two- or three-year stay. If so, make arrangements directly with a building society or finance company yourself; don't negotiate the financing through the estate agent. This can save you the 5 per cent fee the agent receives for arranging financing. (This is in addition to the sales commission.) About one-third of the purchase price is usually required as a down payment; loan rates vary as in the UK.

New construction is exempt from property taxes, but you can expect to pay high installation costs for electricity, water pipes and the like, as well as yearly fees in proportion to your frontage for such things as sewer maintenance. If you buy a flat (quite expensive), your maintenance charges will be relatively low.

ELECTRICITY AND APPLIANCES

German current runs on 220 volts-50 cycles, which means that if you are coming from a country using 110 volts-60 cycles, you will need to think carefully about what appliances to bring with you and what to buy locally.

Foreign nationals throughout Europe recommend that you leave as much electrical equipment behind as you can and buy locally. Since Germany is particularly well known for the quality of its electrical appliances, finding what you want should present no problems. German prices vary from reasonable to expensive, but you can be assured the appliance is built to last. Whatever you buy

Youth hostel accommodation

Germany is very well served by youth hostels. There are well over 500 of them all over the country, offering a bed for about 6 to 10 deutschemarks a night. As is usually the case with youth hostels, there is a set of rules to be observed, for example no consumption of alcohol and tobacco in the premises. You should obtain an international youth hostel membership card before leaving home.

Sources of information
- The annual handbook *Deutsches Jugendherbergsverzeichnis* (Directory of German youth hostels), cost about DM6. Is is published by:
- DJH-Hauptverband, Postfach 20, D-4930 Detmold (the main association of German youth hostels).
- Tourist information office.
- The German Federal Youth Hostel Association, addresses below.

Landesverband Baden
Weinweg 43
D-7500 Karlsruhe
(42 youth hostels)

Landesverband Bayern
Mauerkircher Strasse 5
D-8000 München 80
(110 youth hostels)

Landesverband Berlin
Bayernalle 35
D-1000 Berlin 19
(4 youth hostels)

Landesverband Hannover
Ferd.-Wilh.-Fricke-Weg 1
D-3000 Hannover 1
(58 youth hostels)

Landesverband Hessen
Stegstrasse 3
D-6000 Frankfurt-am-Main
(50 youth hostels)

Landesverband Nordmark
Rennbahnstrasse 10
D-2000 Hamburg
(51 youth hostels)

Landesverband Rheinland
Düsseldorf Strassse 1
D-4000 Düsseldorf
(46 youth hostels)

Landesverband Rheinland-Pfalz
In der Meielache 1
D-6500 Mainz
(45 youth hostels)

Landesverband Schwaben
Urachstrasse 37
D-7000 Stuttgart 1
(40 youth hostels)

Landesverband Unterweser-Ems
Woltmershauser Allee 8
D-2800 Bremen
(58 youth hostels)

Landesverband Westfalen-Lippe
Eppenhauser Strasse 65
D-5800 Westfalen/Hagen
(55 youth hostels)

Other low cost short term accommodation

YMCA/YWCA hostels
In German these acronyms translate to CVJM and CVJF respectively. Branches are to be found in most of Germany's larger towns and cities, though not all have accommodation. To obtain the latest information contact:

- CVJM Gesamtverband in Deutschland e.V., Postfach 410149, Im Druseltal 8, D-3500 Kassel-Wilhelmshöhe;
- The headquarters of the World Alliance of YMCAs at 37 quai Wilson, CH-1201 Geneva, Switzerland.

In addition to the possibilities of accommodation, the local branches can also provide an excellent way of developing social contacts.

University halls of residence
In German, *Studentenwohnheime*. The opportunities are rather limited, however, since German universities tend to be fully occupied all year round. French students may have the best prospects of obtaining such accommodation, by applying for a special French-German ID card. However, there is a university hall of residence in Berlin which will take foreign visitors:

- Wohnheim Hubertusalle, Delbrückstrasse 24, D-1000 33.

Bahnhofsmissionen
The German Travellers' Aid Service located at more than 100 railway stations around the country. Run by volunteers from the churches, they exist to provide information and help for travellers and in some cases can arrange accommodation.

Household Pointers

can be resold before your return home. In fact, a good source of 220 volt-50 cycle appliances is a family returning home.

What you decide to bring and to leave at home will, of course, depend on your family's needs, the age of your equipment, length of stay, and so on, but the following are some general guidelines to help you with your decision.

All 110-volt appliances can be used with a transformer; however, those that must operate at a specific speed (clocks, record players, tape recorders, etc) will have to be adapted to 50 cycles. These are probably best left at home. Television sets are another good candidate for storage at home since European television operates on a different standard. Because a good battery-powered radio is essential, we suggest that you ship your own or plan on buying one (preferably a high-quality shortwave radio) on arrival.

German refrigerators are small, stoves tend to heat slowly, and clothes driers are rare, so you may wish to bring these appliances with you. Since German washing machines heat their own water (only cold water is piped in), it is a good idea to purchase a washing machine locally.

While making decisions about appliances, you may want to consider the following points. German (and European in general) rooms are small, and there is often not enough space for large appliances. Many houses are not wired to carry a heavy load, and electricity is expensive; you can, however, have the local electricity board—which also sells appliances—check your wiring at no cost. And finally, your warranties may not be effective outside the country of purchase. If you do decide to bring your own appliances, be sure to bring spare parts and instruction manuals with you, and bear in mind that you will probably encounter difficulties with repair.

The sizes of the electric plugs in Germany are, as a rule, different from those used in Britain. Sockets have an earth connection and take the standard continental two-pin plug which has an earth strip to match the socket. Light fittings are screw type.

Obtaining a telephone in Germany can be quite an ordeal due to the shortage of phone lines, so try to rent a house or flat with one already installed. Phones are rented, not purchased, and you are charged for installation and billed monthly for your calls. If you cannot take over a phone from the previous tenant, you may have to wait for as long as a year to obtain one. Foreigners are asked for a deposit of about DM 100 upon installation. This deposit can be deducted from your phone bill after six months; don't forget to do so.

HOUSEHOLD HELP

Most expatriates have household help—generally a cleaning woman who comes on a weekly basis. The best way to find help is through neighbours or with their help. Talk with other expatriates, who may recommend their employee to you; or ask the owners of the small local shops if they know of available help. Sometimes wives of EC workers from other countries are looking for domestic work. Local clergy can sometimes be helpful since they know the local residents.

Babysitters are also found by word-of-mouth, through neighbours or through nearby schools and universities. In addition, Europe has a highly developed *au pair* system. An au pair essentially becomes a member of the family, babysitting at night and studying during the day. If you are interested in this kind of arrangement, ask at the local bureau of employment or at the nearest university. Another source of babysitters is the local newspaper. Check the ads or place your own.

Unless you plan on having live-in help from a country outside the EC, you will not need visas or permits for your help. You should, however, check with the local tax board or commune office to determine wage rates, taxes and social security payments that must be paid.

SHOPPING

Supermarkets and department stores are on the increase, but most Germans still do most of their shopping at small specialised shops. You should try to follow their lead. It is an easy way to meet your neighbours and establish relationships with local shopkeepers. You can also practise your German as long as you don't try to shop at peak hours when shopkeepers can't spend much time with you. Some of the most common speciality shops are as follows:

Bäckerei	bakery
Metzgerei, Fleischerei	butcher's shop
Lebensmittelgeschäft	grocer's
Wein und Spirituosen	off-licence
Feinkost	delicatessen

Household Pointers

Buchhandlung — bookshop
Obst- und Gemüseladen — greengrocer's
Kaufhaus, Warenhaus — department store
Herrenbekleidungsgeschäft — men's clothing shop
Damenbekleidungsgeschäft — women's clothing shop
Spielwaren — toy shop
Tabakwarenladen — tobacconist's

Weekly markets, where farmers sell their own produce, are the best—and least expensive—source of fresh produce, jams, pickles, plants, etc. (Health regulations prohibit the touching of fruits and vegetables before they are purchased.)

Buying meat can be a bewildering and often frustrating experience. The following German translations for cuts of meat may be helpful.

Rindfleisch—beef
Hochrippe—prime rib
Filet, Roastbeef—sirloin
Lendenstück—tenderloin
Rumpsteak—sirloin top
Keule mit Hinterhesse—round with rump and shank
Rindskeule—round of beef
Schwanzstück—rump
Keule—leg
Lappen—flank
Bruststück—brisket
Rippenstücke—ribs
Beefsteak—steak

Schweinefleisch—pork
Schulter—shoulder of pork
Vorderschinken—shoulder of ham
Kotelettstücke—loin chops
Lende—loin
Haxen—hocks
Schinken—ham
Schinkenspeck—bacon
Rippenspeere—spare ribs

Hammelfleisch—mutton

Lammenfleisch—lamb
Vorderkeule—shoulder
Koteletten—chops
Nierenstück—roast loin
Brust—breast

Geschäft, Handlung, and *Laden* all mean 'shop'. One shop which might cause you some confusion is the *Drogerie*. The German drugstore sells non-prescription drugs, cosmetics and household goods but no magazines, sweets or cigarettes—and no prescription drugs. To buy prescription drugs, you go to an *Apotheke*. All the *Apotheken* in town take turns being open at night in case of emergency.

The hours and days that the shops are open vary and are often confusing. Some are permitted by law to be open on Sundays; for example, in most cities milk shops are open in the morning, flower shops around noon, and bakeries in the afternoon. Shops generally close at 1400 on Saturdays except for the first Saturday in the month when they remain open until 1800. This variation results from federal laws that were enacted to protect the interests of shop personnel (particularly small shopkeepers who cannot afford the extra staff required to stay open long hours) and to keep working hours within mandated weekly limits.

On entering small shops, you should greet shopkeepers with *Guten Tag* (or in Bavaria, *Grüss Gott*) and, when you leave, say *Auf Wiedersehen*. Don't be surprised if the shopkeeper walks you to the door and opens it for you as you leave. This is a polite gesture, not an attempt to rush you out. In small shops, you normally wait to be helped, but in large shops you may have to ask a salesperson to assist you.

Queuing is not the usual practice, so customers must be rather aggressive about protecting their turn. Because prices are fixed, bargaining is inappropriate. You are expected to carry a shopping bag in which to put your parcels. These are generally small, expandable, and made of string or plastic. If you have forgotten your bag, some will be available for purchase. Browsing in stores is not a common practice; one usually makes the purchase and leaves.

Sales are held twice a year (the end of January and July) and extend over a two-week period. These are end-of-season sales, and prices are reduced substantially. You can find goods at reduced prices during the rest of the year in most shops, marked as *Sonderangebot*. There are also weekly throwaway newspapers which advertise all the local bargains.

If possible, avoid shopping during lunch hour, between 1700 and 1800, and on Saturdays because the shops are most crowded then. In general, you will find the staff in most shops helpful and polite.

Be prepared to watch your diet. Germany is the land of dumplings and strudel, pastries, sausages, cheeses and beer. Although you can get frozen or canned foods from abroad, they are very expensive. The quicker you can shift to the wide variety of local brands, the better. The Germans love to eat, and German food is delicious.

Beverages

You will be able to find whatever you like to drink in Germany. Water is safe almost everywhere and milk is pasteurised, but most Germans prefer to drink wine, beer or bottled mineral water with their meals. Stronger alcoholic drinks such as whisky and martinis are available but are much more expensive than beer or wine.

If wine is your speciality, you will want to become knowledgeable about German wines. Mastering a few fundamentals about the wine regions by which wines are distinguished and classified is the best way to begin; next learn the vineyards and, finally, the vintage years. Many pamphlets and books are available on the subject. Picking the right wine is a real art and a source of great pleasure.

If you are a beer lover, you are probably already familiar with at least a few German beers and you can have a marvellous time trying out the whole range—from light beers to the many heavy and dark varieties. The strongest are called 'exports'. During the business day, you may want to drink *Ausschank*, an excellent, light draught beer. Among the pilsner beers, the best are still from Czechoslovakia although German pilsners have improved considerably. Ask German acquaintances to recommend brands of beer. They love to do so and will often start animated conversations as they discuss the varieties among themselves and tell you the differences.

In German restaurants, beer is served in half-litre glasses (except in Bavaria). In Munich you may find yourself drinking from litre mugs (just under two pints) called *Masskruge*.

MEASUREMENTS

Unless you intend to carry a calculator around with you when you go shopping, you will find dealing with weights and measurements much easier if you think metrically.

1 gram (g)	0.035 oz
1 kilogram (kg) (1000 grams)	2.2 lbs
1 centimetre (cm)	0.3937 in.
2.54 centimetres	1 in.
1 metre (m)	3.280 ft.
1,609.3 metres	1 mile
1 kilometre	0.625 mile
1 litre (l)	1.76 pints
4.546 litres	1 gallon

For conversion of recipes:

4 oz	113 grams
1 teaspoon	5 grams
1 tablespoon	12 grams
1 lb	450 grams
1 Kg	2.2 lbs

Temperature

Fahrenheit	Centigrade (*Celsius*)
100.4	38
95	35
86	30
77	25
69.8	21
50	10
41	5
32	0
23	-5
14	-10
5	-17
1.4	-25

Clothing

Clothing size equivalents are noted on the chart on page 83. Once you have identified your size, there should be no problem in

Household Pointers

finding clothes that fit. Children's sizes generally go by age and/or weight.

Skirts, dresses, coats

British	Continental
10	38
12	40
14	42
16	44
18	46
20	48

Shoes

British	Continental
3½-4	37
4½-5	38
5½-6	39
6½	40
7	41
7½	42
8½	43
9½	44

Shirts

British	Continental
14	36
14½	37
15	38
15½	39
16	41
16½	42
17	43

Suits

British	Continental
36	46
38	48
40	50
42	52
44	54
46	56
48	58

Hats

British	Continental
7	57
7⅛	58
7¼	59
7⅜	60
7½	61

7
Health and Medical Care

Because most of Germany has a moderate climate without extremes in temperature, you will probably not encounter many health problems, except for respiratory difficulties—colds, bronchitis and similar ailments—or rheumatic conditions which are aggravated by the dampness. The quality and purity of the drinking water, dairy products and other foods are strictly controlled by government inspectors. The standards for community sanitation and cleanliness are extremely high.

If you do become ill, you will be in good hands. German health standards are excellent, and the standards in the field of medicine and medical practice are exemplified by their excellent hospitals. They are world leaders in the fields of pharmaceuticals, optics and hearing aids.

Doctors' office hours are normally 1000-1200 and 1600-1700 (except Wednesdays and weekends). Each doctor posts his or her hours in a readily visible place outside the office.

Germany has a competent emergency service. Anyone in need may call *Aertlich Notdienst*, listed in the local telephone directory, for information on and phone numbers for those doctors on call.

HEALTH INSURANCE

Medical costs have risen more sharply in Germany than in other parts of Europe. You may want to look into acquiring state insurance coverage (*Krankenkasse*) if your salary is paid in DMs. Eighty-eight per cent of the population is covered by the plan and report that its services are excellent. Foreign nationals living in Germany are eligible for the benefits of this health insurance plan (see Appendix on Social Security).

All care is free to insured persons, apart from small charges for medicines and for hospital care (further details are given in

Appendix I). This includes professional consultations and medical examinations, surgery, therapy, convalescent care, home nursing, psychotherapy, pharmaceuticals, and dental care (both maintenance and prosthetics) as well as a generous death payment. This is one of the most comprehensive insurance systems in the world. It is under the general supervision of the Federal Ministry of Labour and Social Affairs and is administered through local insurance offices.

The employer and employee each pay half of the insurance payments. Those insured may select their physicians from the membership (most of Germany's doctors and dentists are members of the plan) and may change doctors at any time. They may also choose their hospital, if authorised by the physician, and will have semi-private accommodation unless the illness requires a private room. (Anyone can pay the difference and have a private room.) During a hospitalisation period, the health insurance plan provides a maintenance allowance to meet current expenses. If you have private health insurance in the UK, this insurance may cover your international needs as well. If it does, pay medical bills and submit them along with a description of the treatment for reimbursement.

SPAS

There are more than 250 registered spas, not only featuring modern therapeutic care of all sorts (thermal, mineral, etc.) but also providing entertainment and sports to speed the recuperative process. The cost of three or four days, including treatment, is low.

You can get a list of all-inclusive spa vacations from either of the following: Deutsches Reisebüro GmbH, D 6 Frankfurt/Main, Eschersheimer Landstrasse 25/27 or Deutscher Baederverband, D 53 Bonn, Schumannstrasse 111.

8
Education

INTERNATIONAL OR LOCAL: IT'S YOUR CHOICE

For many children, attending school in another culture is a tremendously valuable experience. At the primary level, most children can adapt successfully to European schools without prior knowledge of the host-country language because the basic curricula are similar and language learning comes more easily to young children. However, European curricula, educational systems, and educational philosophies vary greatly at the secondary school and university levels.

Each alternative has positive and negative aspects. When you and your child(ren) are thinking about local or international schools, consider all the possibilities before making a final decision. School choice is one of the most important decisions you will need to make while you are abroad. This international experience (centred, for your child, in and around his or her prime activity—school) will help set the tone for your child's future.

Prior to making your decision, visit the available schools. With your child(ren), make a list of all the questions and concerns you have regarding each school and its programmes. Try not to judge a school by its lavish or spartan appearance. A school should be considered in the light of many criteria: fulfilment of your child's needs and, of course, personal preference, not to mention affordability.

In choosing a school at any level, you need to consider your child's goals and interests. If your child is especially interested in sports or other extra-curricular activities, the international school will probably be a better match than the local school. Most local education has an academic focus even in the lower grades. If your child learns quickly, is a strong student, and enjoys new challenges, a local school may be a wise choice, allowing for the opportunity to learn and use a second language and a new culture.

If you will be returning to your own country before your children complete secondary school or its equivalent, another consideration is acceptability and transferability of credits. Because of the differences in curricula, teaching methods, and diploma requirements, transferring between national systems is difficult and may result in loss of credit for course work completed. Finding a school offering a compatible curriculum, transferable credits and similar completion requirements can eliminate at least one of the problems your child(ren) may face on returning home.

The following list of questions may help you in making your decision about a local or international school.

Primary
- *Environment:* Is the general atmosphere warm and relaxed or conservative and strict? Do the students seem happy, well adjusted?

- *Facilities:* Is there a library? If so, is it adequate? Is there a gym? Is there a nurse on staff, an infirmary?

- *Curriculum/activities*: What is included in the curriculum at your child's age level? How does this match what he or she has studied? Are music, art and physical education a part of the curriculum? What other activities are available (scouts and guides, team sports, music lessons, etc.)?

- *Parental involvement:* What is the level of parental involvement in classroom activities? Is there a PTA, a school board?

Secondary
- *Costs:* Is there tuition, and if so, what is it and what is included? What additional fees and charges can be expected (excursions, lab fees, etc.)?

- *School population*: What percentage of the students are foreign, what local? What is the average class size? What is the ratio of staff to students?

- *Academic*: What is the academic and national background of

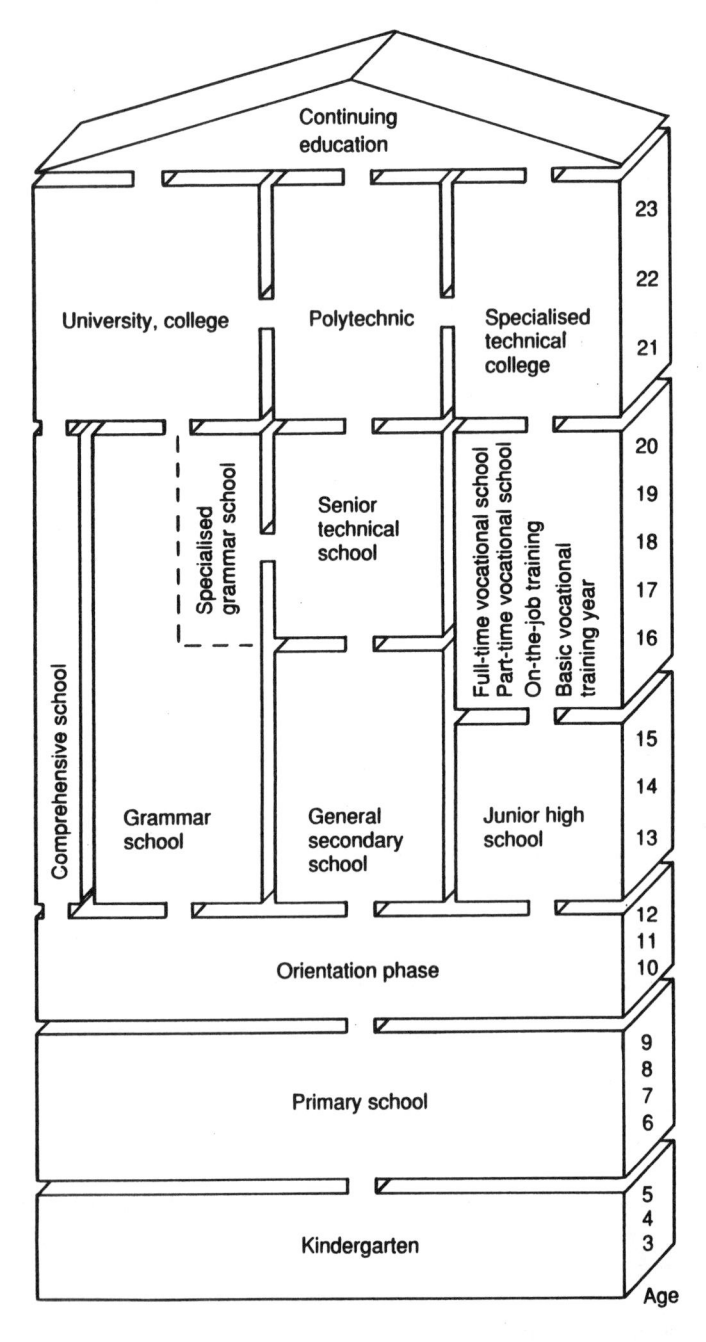

Structure of Germany's education system

the teachers? Are remedial classes offered? Is tutorial help available? Do the majority of graduates go to a college or university, and if so, where? Are credits from the school readily accepted by schools, and/or universities in your home country?

- *Counselling*: Is career and/or college guidance available, and if so, who is responsible for it? What other types of counselling and assistance are available?

- *Activities*: What extra-curricular activities are available? Are there required (optional) trips, and are there additional costs for trips and activities? Are art and music a part of the curriculum?

- *Athletics*: Is physical education a part of the curriculum? What sport are available—team sports, extra-curricular?

- *Student responsibility*: Is cooperative work required/available (library, cafeteria, offices, etc.)? Is there a student government and if so, what is its role and responsibility?

- *Discipline*: What are the school rules and how are infringements handled? What methods of discipline are used? Who is responsible for determining and carrying out disciplinary actions?

GERMAN SCHOOLS

The German school system is excellent. Schools are under the control of the individual states (*Länder*), and curriculum and administrative policies and procedures vary, as do the costs. Public schools are government (state) supported, but fees are charged for some services and activities. School is mandatory only for nine years, and children can repeat every grade if necessary. German private schools are known for their high standards. Some offer classes in English, but most have long waiting lists for entry.

The educational programme consists of an elementary stage and two secondary stages. Although most German children between the ages of three and six attend kindergarten, compulsory education begins at age six and continues until age fifteen. The primary stage includes kindergarten and four years of primary school. Primary schools provide the children with basic knowledge and skills in all the traditional academic subjects.

Class size is usually limited to between twenty and thirty pupils. Five or six class periods per day with different teachers for each subject are the rule. School is dismissed in the early afternoon, but children have a considerable amount of homework.

Secondary education is closely linked to the trades, business or professions that students plan to pursue and is intended to train students to fulfil the needs of society rather than to offer equal educational opportunities for all.

Educational and career decisions are made early, and work experience is considered an important part of the educational process. After the age of ten, the first selective process divides children into three middle-level programmes: *Hauptschule, Realschule,* and *Gymnasium* (some states have an orientation level)—*Orientierungsstufe*—for the first two years at secondary level. Typically Gymnasium leads to university, Realschule to specialized education or technical training, and Hauptschule to vocational training. Selection among the the three options is based on the students' grades and aptitude and on parental preference. As shown in the diagram on page 88, another decision must be made at the age of fifteen or sixteen. At this point, the decision rests not only on performance in school and the interests of the student but on the students' financial resources and on competition through tests and academic achievement for a place in the school of choice. As the diagram suggests, it is possible to continue one's education through any route if the student is determined, is successful in gaining admission, and has the financial resources necessary.

ENGLISH LANGUAGE SCHOOLS

American, British and international schools have been established in most of the major cities in Germany. As you can see from the details given below, most of the international schools are American in style, especially as regards syllabus, etc., which may be a disadvantage for children who will be returning to complete their education in the UK.

The British Embassy in Bonn has a preparatory school for children aged 4 to 13 (British Embassy Preparatory School, D.5300 Bonn 2, Bad-Godesburg-Heiderhof, Tulpenbaumweg). Schools for children of British military personnel will sometimes also accept children of British civilians.

American schools
The following American schools are open to any child—American, host country or international.

John F. Kennedy Schule Berlin, 1000 Berlin 37 (Zehlendorf), Teltower Damm 87-93.

Over 1300 children ranging from kindergarten to thirteenth grade attend this school. Of these about 600 are from the United States, 600 from Germany and about 50 are from other nations. Nearly half of the 100 faculty members are American, and the school follows an American curriculum.

American International School of Düsseldorf, 4000 Düsseldorf 31, Leuchtenberger Kirchweg 2 (or APO New York 09080).

This school includes pre-kindergarten to twelfth grade, with an enrolment of over 300, half of whom are in grades one to six. Of the total student population, about 170 are American, 30 are German and 100 are from other countries. Most of the faculty are American, as is the curriculum.

The Frankfurt International School, 6370 Oberursel/Taunus, An der Waldlust 5-7.

Classes for the nearly 1200 students range from kindergarten through to thirteenth grade. Approximately half of the school's population is American; the remainder of the students are about evenly divided between Germans and other country nationals. Most of the full-time faculty are American, as is the curriculum.

Internationale Schule Hamburg, 2000 Hamburg 52, Holmbrook 20.

Kindergarten through to grade twelve are offered in this school. Of the 550 students, approximately 250 are from the USA; the rest are from Germany and other countries. At least half of the faculty is American, as is the curriculum.

Munich International School, 8136 Percha über Starnberg, Schloss Buchhof.

With grades from kindergarten to twelfth as well as a nursery school programme, this school has an enrolment of over 600 students, mostly American. It offers an American curriculum, supplemented with courses in German language and culture.

English language preschools
American Nursery Play School (ages three to five)—Bonn.
British Embassy Preparatory School (ages 4-13)—Bonn.
Children's Centre (ages thirty-three months to five)—Berlin.
Carl Schurz School (ages three to five)—Frankfurt.
Kindergarten Erbe (ages three to six)—Hamburg.

International schools
The following English-language schools offer either a German or International Baccalaureate Diploma curriculum (see below).

Euregio Gymnasium, Akademie Klausenhof, 4236 Hamminkeln 2, Klausenhofstrasse 100.

Europaische Schule Karlsruhe, 7500 Karlsruhe-Waldstadt, Albert-Schweitzer-Strasse 1.

Europaische Schule München, 8000 München 83, Elisa-Aulinger-Strasse 21.

INTERNATIONAL BACCALAUREATE

Many schools are now offering an International Baccalaureate Diploma (IB) in addition to or instead of UK, USA or other national exams or diplomas. The IB, established in 1971, is the first programme meeting international university entrance requirements and is accepted by most British universities. The two-year IB programme offers a demanding curriculum in the major academic fields. High standards are maintained by means of externally administered, thorough examinations.

The IB programme can provide a challenge for the gifted child, enrich the educational programme of the schools, and facilitate the placement of students in universities in many countries. It is based on the concept of developing 'all the powers of the mind through which people interpret, modify and enjoy their environment'. For some students, the completion of an IB programme may require an additional year of school.

During the two-year programme, the IB diploma candidate must complete the course work and receive acceptable grades in examinations in six subjects, three at higher level and three at subsidiary level. Higher-level subjects require at least five periods of instruction per week for two years while subsidiary-level subjects require five hours per week for one year or three hours per week for two years. The required courses for completion of the IB diploma programme are the following:

1. Language A (generally the students' native language).
2. Language B (a second language).
3. Study of humanity (one of the following): history, geography, economics, philosophy, psychology, social anthropology.
4. Experimental sciences (one of the following): biology, chemistry, physics, physical science.
5. Mathematics.
6. One of the following: art, music, a third language, a second subject under number 3 or 4, or further mathematics.

The International Baccalaureate programme is a structured programme offering a strong general education as well as being flexible and acknowledging the individuality of the student.

UNIVERSITIES

Germany's thirty-one universities are lively centres of activity, as are its nine technical institutions and one hundred music, theological and other post-secondary schools. Foreign students wishing to enrol for higher education programmes must have a secondary education certificate which is recognised in the Federal Republic. In certain cases they are required to complete a preparation course at a 'Kolleg', but all must have sufficient command of the German language. Information on higher education courses and admission requirements can be obtained from the German Academic Exchange Service (*see* Useful Addresses section at the end of this book). You should note that enrolment is not easy for foreigners because German university students are faced with tightened admissions requirements. Many are being turned away due to lack of facilities.

Universities are an excellent source for finding someone with whom to exchange practice in German and English. There will probably also be a large number of German students who have studied in English-speaking countries and who may be delighted to brush up on their English skills or just meet a family from the country where they studied. If you have teenagers, inviting English-speaking German students to your home can create a bridge for your young people into university student circles and perhaps launch them into a lifelong friendship.

Among the many students from other countries at the universities in Germany, you can find many English speakers who are eager to make friends—to practise their English or to have access to home life (students can be lonely and homesick).

STUDYING IN GERMANY

There are 238 university institutions in West Germany, including universities, specialist colleges and the relatively new *Fachhochschulen* (Polytechnics). It's a country with strong academic traditions and may 'centres of excellence' for research espcially in scientific and technological fields. In addition the Goethe Institutes and many private language schools provide a wealth of opportunities for learning German language and culture.

The academic year is divided into two semesters, starting in October and April.

Best contacts for information
- German Academic Exchange Service (*Deutscher Akademischer* Austauschdienst, DAAD), 17 Bloomsbury Square, London WC1A. Tel (071) 404 4065.
- DAAD Headquarters, Kennedyallee 50, D-5300 Bonn 2, and branches throughout the world.

1st degree courses

Studies at German universities are divided into two stages—the first consists of foundation studies after which an Intermediate Examination gives access to a second stage of more specialised studies. The degrees obtained after this second period are the *Magister Artium* (Arts and Humanities) and the *Diplom* (Social and Natural Sciences), which are normally regarded as equivalent to our Master's degrees.

Length
Most degree courses are scheduled to last about four years, but students have considerable freedom in choice of course components

and present themselves for examination only when they think they are ready to take them, so it may take much longer than this to actually obtain the degree.

Contact
The **Akademische Auslandsämter** (Foreign Student Services) of each university. The DAAD (see above) can provide a booklet *Studies at Universities* which lists these, as well as providing detailed information about study in Germany.

Entrance requirements
The equivalent of the *Abiter* (ie 'A' levels) plus a very good knowledge of German. In some cases students are required to complete a preparatory course at a *Kolleg*—the DAAD can supply information on this. No formal qualifications are required for art and music colleges.

Cost/grants
Tuition is free, but living expenses—especially accommodation—are high; no scholarships are generally available for foreigners for first degrees, so some means of support are necessary.

Postgraduate
Contact The Akademische Auslandsämter of each institution as above.

Entrance requirements
Usually a Master's degree in order to enrol for a doctorate (*Promotion*—the next degree after a *Magister* or *Diplom*) and, again, excellent German.

Grants
As with first degrees, tuition is free, but at postgraduate level various institutions offer grants for study and research. The DAAD booklet *Studies at Universities* (see above) lists an appendix of 'Institutions in the Federal Republic of Germany that provide Financial Aid to Foreign Students'.

The DAAD itself offers up to 15 postgraduate scholarships annually to British citizens with a good knowledge of German for study at German institutions in any field. It also offers short term (one to four months) research grants to PhD students or post-doctoral research workers. Apply through the DAAD office in London.

The Ministry of Education of the Rhineland-Palatinate offers one scholarship annually at the University of Mainz. Again British nationality and a good knowledge of German are essential. Apply through the British Council, Hahnenstrasse 6, D-5000 Köln 1.

The Alexander von Humbolt Foundation offers a large number of post-doctoral fellowhips to German speakers from all countries. Further information from Alexander von Humboldt-Stiftung, Jean-Paul-Strasse 12, D-5300 Bonn 2.

The King Edward VII British-German Foundation offers two or three postgraduate scholarships annually, tenable at any West German institution in any subject. Apply to The Secretary, King Edward VII British-German Foundation, 50 Hamilton Avenue, Pyford, Woking, Surrey GU22 8RU.

International University
The independent Schiller International University has a branch in Heidelberg, offering Bachelors and Masters degrees in liberal arts, European studies, economics, languages, business administration etc—in English. For further details apply to Schiller International University, Friedrich-Ebert-Anlage 4, D-6900 Heidelberg.

Visiting studentships
Apply through the Akademisches Auslandsamt at each university.

Language courses
The Goethe-Instituts (16 in West Germany, 4 in the UK and a further 145 throughout the world) are universally recognized in the field of German as a Foreign Language. Their leaflet *Deutschlernen* gives full details of the many courses they run in Germany; it also includes an application form to be sent to their Head Office in Munich for central processing: Goethe-Institut, Lenbachplatz 3, D-8000 München 2. Tel (010 4989) 5999-200. There are Goethe-Instituts in Berlin, Bonn, Boppard, Bremen, Düsseldorf, Frankfurt, Freiburg, Göttingen, Iserlohn, Mannheim, Munich, Murnau, Prien, Rothenburg, Schwäbisch Hall and Staufen; central processing of applications means that if there are no places on your first choice of centre you can be assigned to another. For the leaflet mentioned above and any other queries, apply to one of the Goethe-Instituts in Britain:

50 Prince's Gate, Exhibition Road, London SW7 2PH. Tel (071) 581 3344.
Ridgefield House, 14 John Dalton Square, Manchester M2 6JR. Tel (061) 834 4635.
The King's Manor, Exhibition Square, York YO1 2EP. Tel (0904) 55222.
Scottish-German Centre, Lower Medway Building, 74 Victoria Crescent Road, Glasgow G12 9SC. Tel (041) 334 6116.

Language courses are also run by universities, partly as summer schools (see below) and partly for intending or current students who do not have German as a first language. In addition there are many private language schools big and small; details of these appear in the Central Bureau's guide *Study Holidays*. Large organizations such as Berlitz, Inlingua, Eurocentres and International House each have several centres. The organization Deutsch in Deutschland (head office Hauptstrasse 26, 8751 Stockstadt/Main, tel Stockstadt 20090) has 27 schools throughout the Federal Republic. Some courses may be booked through agents or offices in Britain.

Cultural and Educational Services Abroad
Euro-Academy
Eurocentres
International House
International Study Programmes

School Journey Association, 48 Cavendish Road, London SW12 0DG. Tel (081) 673 4849.

See also the Organisation für Internationale Kontakte, Postfach 201051, D-5300 Bonn 2. Tel (010 49228) 357013.

Summer schools

The following institutions run International Summer Schools, each lasting about a month, in German language, literature, culture and society:

- Albert-Ludwigs University, Heinrich-von-Stephen-Strasse 25, D-7800 Freiburg im Breisgau.
- Christian-Albrechts University, Olshausenstrasse 40-60, D-2300 Kiel.
- Trier University, Postfach 3825, D-5500 Trier.
- University of Bonn, Office for Foreign Academic Affairs, Nassestrasse 15, D-5300 Bonn.
- University of Munster, Schlossplatz 2, D-4400 Munster.

- University of Regensburg, Universitätstrasse 31, D-8400 Regensburg.

There are also Musical Summer Schools (for music students or professional musicians) at the following:
- Musikalische Jugend Deutschland, Markplatz 12, D-6992 Weikersheim.
- Internationales Musikinstitut Darmstadt, Nieder-Ramstädter Strasse 190, D-6100 Darmstadt.

Exchange Scholarships
Various German institutions offer Exchange Scholarships for students enrolled at British universities (applications should generally be made through the home university):
—Christian-Albrechts University, Olshausenstrasse 40-60, D-2300 Kiel.
—Free University of Berlin, Altensteinstrasse 40, D-1000 Berlin 33.
—Ruprecht-Karls-Universität, Seminarstrasse 2, Postfach 105760, D-6900 Heidelberg 1 (with Universities of Cambridge and Sussex only).
—University of Bonn, Nassestrasse 15, D-5300 Bonn 1.

Welfare
All students have to pay a welfare contribution (between 20 and 60 marks per semester) to the Student Welfare Organisation (**Studentenwerk**) which covers the cost of various services it provides. Health insurance is automatically covered for EC students.

Useful addresses
German National Tourist Office, 61 Conduit Street, London W1R 0EN. Tel (071) 734 2600.

Student travel
German Student Travel Service, Terminal House, Lower Belgrave Street, London SW1W 0NP. Tel (071) 730 2101.
   ARTU, Hardenbergstrasse 9, D-1000 Berlin 12.
   RDS, Rentselstrasse 17, D-2000 Hamburg 13.
   Asta-Reisen, Keplerstrasse 17, K2 Stuttgart 1.
   STR, Wilhelmstrasse 30, D-7400 Tübingen.
   Federal Ministry for Education and Science, Heinemannstrasse 2, D-5300 Bonn 2.

9
Cars and Driving

SPEED LIMITS AND ROAD SIGNS

Nearly everyone has heard of Germany's famous autobahns, where drivers push their cars to breakneck speeds, but a lot of people who visit Germany are not aware of the many other scenic highways with reasonable speed limits. The basic regulations regarding speed limits are 50 km/h (30 mph) in cities and 100 km/h (60 mph) on all other roads except autobahns, where there is now a recommended limit of 130 km/h (about 80 mph). If no speed limit is posted, don't be fooled into thinking there is no limit—the limit is 50 km/h! In spite of set limits, it is always wise to let the weather, traffic and road conditions determine when lower speeds are appropriate.

Driving is on the right, and road signs follow the international system. Drive and walk with extreme caution in Germany. The accident rate is so high that the government is clamping down severely on speeding and drunken driving. Speeders, if caught, must pay stiff fines, and drunken driving may result in imprisonment along with fines. The death toll has been appalling—50 per cent more deaths per capita on the road than in Britain and 150 per cent more than in the USA.

For information about speed traps, fines and regulations, consult Shell's *German Road Atlas* or AA or RAC guides to driving in Europe. You are, for example, required to keep seatbelts fastened in a car. A folder, entitled 'Autobahn Service', shows the entire autobahn system and the location of service facilities and is available in English at roadhouses, service stations and border crossings.

THE BIG QUESTION: TO IMPORT OR BUY LOCALLY?

You will most likely want to own a car during your stay in Germany, not only for your exploration of Germany but for travelling throughout Europe. This poses an immediate question: is it better to import your current car (owned three months or more) into Germany or to buy a German car?

You may prefer to take your own car if you think you would find it difficult to adjust to a left-hand drive vehicle. Against this may be set the problem of spares and repairs if it is not a car commonly driven in the Federal Republic.

If you are taking up permanent residence in Germany, you should be able to import your car free of all customs charges, as it will be considered part of your 'household goods'. This only applies, however, if your car is for your personal use or to enable you to carry out your business, trade or profession, and as long as you do not aim to sell the car immediately after your arrival.

All imported cars (belonging to those planning to live in Germany more than one year) must be inspected by the German Technical Inspection Team (*Technischer Überwachungsverein* or TUV). This is done immediately after arrival to assure roadworthiness and again after two years. Imported cars may have to undergo certain modifications to conform to existing German laws.

If you buy a car in Germany, your savings may be considerable, especially if you drive it locally before shipping it home on your return. There are time restrictions, however, so investigate the laws carefully. By buying locally, you may also avoid import duties and taxes, expensive alterations to meet German requirements, and the hassle of trying to sell an imported car before you leave. Should you choose this alternative, you will be given export papers at the time you take delivery of the car. These papers must remain in your possession until you deliver the car to a shipping agent for its export to your home country.

Renting a car

If your stay in Germany will be a short one, or if you will be living in an urban area with adequate public transport, renting a car may be a viable option. There is no lack of reliable rental firms. Among them are Hertz, Avis, Autohansa, Auto Sixt and Europa Service. Rental costs vary according to the size and make of the car; mileage and petrol are extra. If you are eligible for a discounted rate at home, be sure to enquire at the German rental agency—it might apply in Germany also.

REGULATIONS

If you are going to live in Germany for more than a year, you need to obtain a German driving licence by applying to the responsible licensing authority at least three months before the end of the year.

Your application must be accompanied by:

- your passport;
- a passport-size photograph;
- a valid foreign driving licence (and a certified translation unless the licence was issued in an EC country);
- a certificate stating that you meet eyesight requirements.

You will have to carry third-party liability insurance (*Haftpflichtversicherung*). This is arranged through a German insurance company. A statement from your home insurance company attesting to your accident-free driving record may greatly reduce your insurance premium in Germany. The premium will be based on your driving record and on the car's horsepower. You will also need to provide proof of car ownership and of registration (if the car is imported). A motor vehicle cannot be operated in Germany until it is registered by the *Strassenverkehrsamt*, the equivalent of the Department of Transport. The applicant must pay a motor vehicle tax (road tax) and provide proof of liability insurance and vehicle inspection.

If you plan to drive outside Germany, you must have a nationality plate on the car and an international licence. Information and regulations about international driving are readily available at any of the German automobile clubs. For this reason (and many others), joining an automobile club makes sense. If you are a member of the AA or RAC, some services may be available to you from European automobile clubs.

GERMAN AUTOMOBILE CLUBS

German automobile clubs operate highway patrols and provide free service on all major highways for their members. The three automobile clubs in Germany are as follows:

1. ADAC: Allgemeiner Deutscher Automobil Club, D 8 München 22, Königstrasse 9-11A.
2. AVD: Automobilclub von Deutschland, D 6 Frankfurt-Niederrad, Lyonerstrasse 16.
3. DTC: Deutscher Touring Automobil Club, D 8 München 60, Elisabethstrasse 30.

Non-members may use their services but must pay a fee. ADAC (one of the larger organisations) also provides this service within major cities and operates rental services for tyre chains in the mountain areas. It publishes an annual detailed camping guide as well.

10
Adult Leisure

MEETING GERMANS

It is possible to live in Germany as if you had never left home, but you will return home with few new experiences, and you will miss an opportunity for personal enrichment and real contact with a rich and wonderful culture and warm, friendly people. Meeting Germans is not difficult, but it will take some effort on your part and it is necessary to work at learning and using their language.

There are numerous ways to meet Germans informally; approachable and easygoing, they will wait for you to take the initiative rather than intruding on you. The more you try to speak German, the easier meeting Germans will be. Everyone will nod and smile and give you an encouraging '*ja, ja, ja*' as you struggle to get out a sentence. It is important to remember that while only a little initiative is necessary for meeting and becoming acquainted, a considerable amount of time and effort goes into establishing a friendship.

Take part in sports; join in when there are festivals; drink beer in *Ratskeller*—sit at the long tables with others and join in the songs, even if you only hum along; talk to and ask informed questions of people you meet in parks, at museums and on trips. Many lifelong friendships between British people and Germans have begun on sightseeing buses, trains, and at country inns.

There are also Rotary and Lions clubs throughout Germany; check with your clubs at home for German counterparts.

The British Chamber of Commerce in Germany (see *Useful Addresses*) organises meetings, discussion groups, workshops and social events for business people in many cities throughout the Federal Republic.

You will also make acquaintances and connections through

participation in the activities of your children's schools and scout troops or your church.

If you are a university graduate, you may want to get in touch with the University Graduates club (men) or the Association of University Women. These groups bring together people from many cultures, who meet to hear interesting speakers and to participate in organised trips.

If you move to a large city where there is a consulate or embassy, you should drop in, pay your respects, and make your presence known. The embassy or consulate is often a good source of information about activities or channels through which you can meet local people. Don't expect a great deal of assistance, however, since the consulates are not prepared to provide services for expatriates.

SPORTS

The Germans are an athletic and vigorous people. All kinds of sports activities are popular and readily available. Camping, biking and hiking are long-standing favourites, and so are the many different kinds of mechanised racing. Germans love speed and turn out in droves for car, motorbike, speedboat or bicycle racing.

Other popular sports include polo, tennis, ice hockey, gliding and horse racing. Another popular sport is fencing, and Germany is a wonderful place to learn it because the Germans are among the world's best fencers. Skiing and ice-skating are winter favourites; there are some three hundred ski resorts in Germany alone, not to mention those in Switzerland, France or Scandinavia, all easily reached by short plane or pleasant train rides.

Hostelling

Germany is well known for its youth hostels, 750 of which dot the landscape. Many are in historic castles and monasteries. Walking or riding a bicycle from one hostel to another along the old roads, canals or rivers is an experience to be savoured. And anyone can do it—from teenagers to the young at heart. It is an excellent way to experience Germany, to meet a cross-section of Europeans, and to make new friends. For further information contact Deutsches Jugendherbergswerk, D-493 Detmold, Bülowstrasse 26.

Golf
A guide to Germany's golf courses is published each year in German by Golf und Sportverlag, Horst Ostermann, D 6202 Wiesbaden-Bieberich, Rudolf-Vogt-Strasse 1.

Sailing
Germany's many lakes and hundreds of miles of coast make it ideal for sailing, and lessons for the novice are readily available. For information contact the German Yachting Association, D 2 Hamburg 22, Schwanenwik 27. Another useful address is Verband Deutscher Segelschulen, D 44 Münster, Bottshaus am Aasee. If you are a sailing buff, be sure not to miss the big Regatta Week each year at Kiel.

Fishing
Lake, river, stream and deep-sea fishing are available, but you will need two licences: state and owner's. For information contact Verband Deutscher Sportfischer, D 605 Offenbach, Waldstrasse 6.

Hiking and climbing
The Verband Deutscher Gebirgs und Wandervereine (Germany's chief hiking and climbing organisation) is composed of forty-seven clubs with two thousand local chapters and three hundred thousand members. Contact the organisation for more information: D 7 Stuttgart, Hospitalstrasse 21 b.

The German Alpine Association operates 239 huts, which are open to all climbers; members receive a 50 per cent discount. The association's address is Alpenvereinshaus, D 8 München, 5 Praterinsel, 22.

Walking
If you enjoy walking, the *Volksmarch* will delight you. The Volksmarch is an organised walk along a marked trail that may skirt private gardens, cut through farms, follow forest paths, or meander along village streets—often all of the above. There are control points (*Kontrolle*), where you will receive light refreshments (pratically a full meal) and a progress stamp on your pass. The final stamp is available at the finish (*Ziel*). The rates are reasonable, and the walks offer a unique view of the countryside and of the Germans.

The German National Association (DVV) is an umbrella organisation for over 1,700 separate 'wandering' clubs. Altogether, these clubs sponsor as many as 1,600 Volksmarch events each year. Joining a club will ensure that you receive a calendar of events, record books and other materials. For more information, contact DVV-Geschäftsstelle, 8262 Altötting, Fabrikstrasse 8.

Flying

If flying is your sport, you will find ample opportunity to take to the skies. The Aero Club, at D 6 Frankfurt, Lyonerstrasse 16, has a thousand branches. A list of flying schools is available from the German Tourist Office in any major city.

THE ARTS

Theatre

The Germans love the theatre and support some 190 active theatres in approximately four hundred cities and towns, some of which are run for and by workers in connection with trade unions. No matter where you are in Germany, you will probably be within fifty miles of a theatre, where a wide range of the world's great dramas—Russian, Italian, British, Irish, American, ancient Greek, and prize-winning German works—are being presented. In the summer, dramas are presented in spectacular outdoor settings. In fact, theatre may be your greatest incentive for learning the German language. Curtain time at most theatres is 2000, sometimes earlier. Tickets normally go on sale ten days in advance of the opening, starting on a Saturday, and may be purchased at ticket offices at various locations in the larger cities as well as at theatre box offices. The hotel concierge is often a good source of information about tickets.

Cinema

Film production is relatively new for Germany; even so, German directors are producing fine films whose quality is recognised throughout the world. Many British and American films are shown with German sound tracks or subtitles—an ideal way to practise the language. There is also an interesting selection of films from Italy, Sweden, Czechoslovakia and other countries.

Music

Germans are especially fond of music. Every major city has its own philharmonic orchestra, and sixty-three cities have permanent opera and ballet companies. Annual festivals abound; some of the best known are at Bayreuth, München, Berlin and Wiesbaden. Popular operetta is performed from the end of June to mid-September on a floating stage at Koblenz. All in all, there is music for all tastes. To make sure you don't miss your favourites, get a calendar of events from the nearest German Tourist Office.

Miscellaneous

If you have never lived abroad before, you may not realise that reading is an important pastime. Although English-language books can be obtained (at a high price), the selection may not meet your interests. You can order books from catalogues, and you may want to join a book club before leaving home to ensure a steady supply of reading material.

If you enjoy do-it-yourself projects, you will find excellent tools at your disposal. Gardening is very popular among the Germans and supplies are abundant. If music is your hobby, you will find musical instruments for rent at moderate prices. There is very little, in fact, that you cannot find to help you pursue those activities that you enjoy or have always wanted to learn or try.

TRAVEL

For the real flavour of Germany and German hospitality, stop at a hostel, guesthouse (*Gasthaus*) or inn when you travel. You may find yourself staying in a converted castle, a chapel, a timbered inn or a medieval monastery. Picturesque, comfortable, clean, inexpensive and delightful, such low-cost accommodation is a bargain, and meals are included. If you don't want to plan your accommodation in advance, an accommodation bureau (*Zimmernachweis*), located at every railroad station and airport in Germany, can help you find local hotels with vacancies.

Wherever you decide to stay, be it a hotel, inn, manor house, hotel or pension, you will find that rooms with private baths are about 50 per cent dearer than rooms without. This goes for most of the rest of Europe as well. Always take your own face-cloths and soap as these are considered as personal as toothbrushes and are rarely supplied (even in private homes). The smart European tourist also carries toilet paper since many public toilets are not equipped with it.

If you prefer to travel the *autobahns*, you will find good restaurants and motels along the way as well as emergency telephones every mile or so.

One thing you will notice when travelling in Germany is the special clothing seen in villages during local festivals. The clothing is often particular to specific localities; for example, *Lederhosen* and *Dirndl* dresses, usually considered typically German, are really Bavarian. These and other colourful, often very elaborate, costumes will most likely appear at events such as *Karnival, Fasching* (pre-Lenten celebrations) or local festivals.

Camping

Camping is almost a national sport. If you are interested, get the official guide of the Deutscher Camping Club, which is called *Campingführer*. This guide lists some three thousand camping sites in Germany and twenty other countries. Filled with quantities of information, including symbols explained in English, it is available at bookstores and sporting goods shops or you can order it directly from Deutscher Camping Club e.V., 8 München 23, Mandelstrasse 28.

11
Major Cities

BREMEN/BREMERHAVEN

Located at the end of the Weser Estuary, Bremen is the oldest maritime city in Germany; it was a key international trading port in the fifteenth century. Still one of the world's greatest ports, Bremen handles about 10 per cent of Germany's foreign trade. Most of its working population is employed either in port-connected jobs (40 per cent) or in industry.

Bremerhaven, thirty-seven miles downstream, was founded in 1827 as a deep-sea port for Bremen. Together they form an outstanding commercial port system—half the German fishing fleet is based in Bremerhaven.

Housing

The newest section of Bremen lies on the west bank of the river. It is extremely modern, with large apartment blocks and shopping centres. Just beyond the old city, to the east, is the new satellite town of Neue Vahr. Its blocks of flats, broad boulevards, and modern office buildings give it a contemporary and welcoming atmosphere. Commuter transport from these suburban areas is good. As in most German cities, housing is scarce and difficult to locate, so it may take quite some time to find a place to live.

Leisure activities

You will not suffer from a lack of interesting activities during your stay in this area. All water sports are popular, and various international yachting regattas are held here. You will find several golf courses; indoor and outdoor tennis and swimming facilities, many of which are open to the public; riding clubs; football clubs;

and both fishing and hunting (bear, deer, hare, duck and geese). Bremen's six-day bicycle race is world-famous.

Spend time exploring the old town of Bremen on the east bank of the Weser, where you will discover what was once a walled city in the Middle Ages. You can still see the location of the moat that once surrounded the city, now an attractive park that includes Rampart Walk. One old street (a street of crafts even long ago) called Bottcherstrasse is filled with galleries and practising craftspeople. Throughout the year the Stadthalle offers high quality shows featuring internationally known stars. Several museums and galleries are noteworthy:

1. the Übersee Museum, famous for its demonstrations of the various skills and crafts of the peoples of northern Germany;
2. the Focke Museum, specialising in the rich history of the region;
3. the Kunsthalle, featuring a remarkable collection of nineteenth- and twentieth-century German and French art;
4. the National Maritime Museum in Bremerhaven, which traces German maritime history from its beginnings. During the summer, visitors may explore seven ships moored at an open-air exhibit, which is part of the Maritime Museum.

Short trips to the surrounding countryside will take you to prehistoric Wildeshausen; the artist colony of Worpswede; sunny, though chilly, Cuxhaven beach; the upper Weser River or the North Sea for fishing; and the Harz Mountains for skiing.

Clothes
Cold, damp and windy sums up Bremen's weather, so wool or other heavy, warm clothing is essential: warm trousers, jumpers, suits, anoraks, coats and boots. Warm nightclothes and underwear are a necessity. Since the Germans economise on heating fuel (which has become astronomically expensive in Europe), you will find bedrooms and hallways cooler than individual offices and those rooms in homes used by the entire family during the day. Because of this, dressing so that you can add or remove clothing (layering) is both practical and commonplace.

Some useful addresses
Bremen Tourist Association (Verkehrsverein Bremen), 2800 Bremen Tivoli-Hochhaus, Bahnhofsplatz 29.

Local Tourist Office (Verkehrsamt), 2850 Bremerhaven, Friedrich-Ebert-Strasse 58.

DÜSSELDORF

Düsseldorf is the busiest port on the Rhine, a centre for East-West trade and transport, and its airport is one of the busiest in Europe. Some 700,000 people live in the city; a total of 9 million live within fifty kilometres. There is a constant flow of tourists and visitors. In spite of this, the city maintains a small-town feeling. Düsseldorf is a city for people—lively and full of activity—yet it offers an open, relaxed atmosphere, due partly to the Rhine River, which flows through the middle of town, and partly to its extensive parks, like the Hofgarten, and its stately boulevards. Careful planning has preserved the residential character of the city while allowing for industrial expansion.

Known as the 'desk of the Ruhr', Düsseldorf boasts the second largest stock exchange in Germany, houses over five hundred commercial institutions, and served as a major banking centre long before the Rothschilds opened their first offices there. Over forty-four countries maintain consulates in Düsseldorf, and it is the site of Japan's largest overseas trade centre. A trade fair of some sort is almost always in progress at the enormous complex on the northern edge of the city.

The city blends old and new ideas rather easily in a cosmopolitan setting. Because it was a vital port area, the city was heavily damaged during the Second World War, and it looks like a new city due to massive postwar reconstruction. As the capital of North Rhine-Westphalia, it is the location of the State Parliament. It is also a university town with a new campus, built in 1965, drawing many young people to the city. A leader in the arts, Düsseldorf attracts many artists—actors, film-makers, musicians, painters and fashion designers. A city with a diverse population, nearly half of its residents (46 per cent) have come from other cities or countries in the past twenty-five years. The annual Düsseldorf fashion show is said to be the largest in the world, and the city is a shopper's paradise. The Germans call it *die heitere Stadt* (the happy city), and it is indeed a city to enjoy.

Leisure activities

Sports activities and facilities are numerous: indoor and outdoor tennis courts (hard courts at the Rhine Stadium, which has many facilities for sports), skating and ice-hockey rinks, swimming and fishing at nearby Lake Unterback, riding schools, polo clubs, eighteen-hole golf courses, football, bowling, billiards and boccie (a game of Italian origin similar to lawn bowling) are among those from which you may choose.

At the heart of Düsseldorf is the Königsallee (the 'Ko'), which follows a portion of the moat that once surrounded the old town. Along the Ko are cafés, restaurants, luxury shops and a great deal of activity. The Ko leads to the Hofgarten, a lovely park with a number of charming fountains. You can stroll in the old town or visit the many fine museums located here. The Rhineland-Westphalia Collection at the Jägerhof Castle includes works by the twentieth-century artists Klee, Chagall, Kandinsky and Picasso. The Goethe Museum displays pictures of the writer as well as first editions of his works and other memorabilia. Trips along the Rhine are popular, as are the drives to ancient castles, such as the Chateau of Dyck and the Chateau of Rheydt.

Some useful addresses
British Consulate-General, 4000 Düsseldorf 30, Nordsternhaus, Georg-Glock-Strasse 14

Chamber of Industry and Commerce in Düsseldorf, Berliner Allee 10

Tourist and Trade Promotion Office, Ehrenhof 3

Association of Cultural Organisations, Heinrich Heine Allee 49-51

The Brucke-International Educational Centre (School for Extra-mural Studies), Heinrich Heine Allee 49-51

Youth Hostel, Düsseldorfstrasse 1

FRANKFURT AM MAIN

Cosmopolitan Frankfurt is a modern, prosperous city with a population of about 700,000 and a history dating from A.D. 834. Unfortunately, the old city is now only a small, largely reconstructed area around the Romerberg Square. Here you will find the Romer, with fifteenth-century burghers' houses, the Baroque Sallhof (once an imperial palace), and other historic sites. Frankfurt's cathedral (*Dom*) has played an important role in German history as far back as the Holy Roman Empire. German emperors were crowned in the cathedral for many centuries.

Because of its central location, Frankfurt is a huge transport junction for air traffic (third largest airport in Europe), railway and road traffic, and autobahns which converge here from every direction.

Frankfurt also has the distinction of being the financial and commercial capital of the Federal Republic. The Frankfurt Stock Exchange, which leads all others in Germany, is located at Borsenplatz, together with the Chamber of Industry and Commerce and many trade organisations. Frankfurt hosts trade fairs, book fairs and industrial exhibitions in huge numbers. The Exhibition Grounds cover 360,000 square metres and house modern exhibition centres, foreign pavilions, the Congress Hall and the Festival Hall.

No European city has shaped itself so much in the American image as Frankfurt. Largely rebuilt after the Second World War, its skyscrapers, subways and supermarkets mirror those of American cities. Local residents, though, are not entirely satisfied with their American-style city and regret the loss of its German identity.

Housing

Situated on both sides of the Main River, Frankfurt offers a variety of neighbourhoods and lifestyles to newcomers.

Residential areas north of the river receive high ratings from foreign residents. Accommodation ranges from three-room flats with kitchen and bath to two-storey townhouses and luxury bungalows. There is generally a larger selection of homes here than elsewhere in the city. Rents, however, are no different from those in the rest of Frankfurt—high. Connections to the city are excellent: U-bahn, bus and tram. In fact, transport throughout Frankfurt is good.

South of the river, the area of Niederrad is appealing because of convenient connections to the autobahns and Frankfurt International Airport. For relaxation there are peaceful wooded areas, Frankfurt's only golf course, the race track, a large football stadium, and plenty of paths for walking the dog or jogging.

Bordering Niederrad is Sachsenhausen; its colourful apple wine festivals and flea markets make it an enjoyable spot to visit.

Frankfurt's 155,000 commuters, many of them expatriates, find the train service excellent and the rents between 10 and 15 per cent lower in the outlying suburbs. Among choice locations are Wiesbaden, Darmstadt and Oberursel.

Shopping centres have sprung up in strategic locations for the convenience of suburban shoppers. One is the Taunus Zentrum, southwest of Wiesbaden, just off the autobahn in the suburb of Höchst. Another great attraction in the otherwise industrial Höchst is Jahrhunderthalle (Century Hall), which draws renowned performers in both classical and contemporary theatre and all kinds of music.

Leisure activities
Frankfurters are rightfully proud of their parks, especially the Stadtwald, a wooded area covering almost 11,000 acres within the city limits—a lovely area for children and adults alike. Within the Stadtwald is the Waldstadium, a track for cyclists, a swimming pool, tennis courts, an ice-skating rink, and various sports halls. The Frankfurt Zoo is world-famous, known for its rare species and natural animal habitats.

The city operates a number of theatres and the Opera House. Its wholesale market (Ruckerstrasse 6) is one of the largest in Europe, a source of the freshest fruits, vegetables and flowers. The Senckenberg Museum is famous for its Flemish Primitive and sixteenth-century German paintings. Frankfurt is the birthplace of Goethe. His home, reconstructed after the war, and the adjoining Goethe Museum are open to the public.

Since Frankfurt is a major transport hub, it is easy to travel northwest to places like the holiday town of Rudesheim, the charming city of Koblentz, and Köln, with its magnificent cathedral. You can take a delightful cruise along the Rhine, viewing the castles, vineyards and villages along its shores. To the north lies Kassel, with the Hercules statue towering over the park, fountains, and the Chateau of Wilhelmshohe (now a fine museum). Also to the north is Marburg, where half-timbered houses cluster around a hill crowned by the medieval castle that dominates the town. To the south lies Heidelberg, the oldest university town in Germany and a well-known cultural centre.

Useful addresses
British Consulate-General, 6000 Frankfurt am Main, Bockenheimer Landstrasse 51-53

Tourist Office, facing track 23 in the railway station (called Frankfurter Verkehrsverein); provides information and advice in English about housing, theatre, concerts, sports, local facilities, the area, babysitters, and almost anything; also a source for tickets to sports and cultural events

MÜNCHEN (MUNICH)

München, the third largest city in Germany and the largest city in Bavaria, was settled by monks in the eighth century; hence the name *München*, meaning 'home of the monks'. Almost 1.3 million people live in the 12-square-mile valley situated 1,700 feet above sea level. Despite its twelve-hundred-year history, München is new in many respects because so much of it had to be restored after the Second World War. Much of the rebuilt area is along grandiose lines, showing considerable Italian influence.

The city is young in another sense too, for over 40 per cent of its residents are under the age of thirty-five. Roughly 50,000 are students at the University of Munich, the College of Technology, the School of Fine Arts, or the Bavarian State Academy of Music. München is also home to an active international community of more than 200,000 foreigners. In addition, tourists flock there during both summer and winter to enjoy the surrounding mountains and lakes and the Bavarian atmosphere. Many people consider it Germany's loveliest, liveliest and most enjoyable city.

München has attracted a diversity of business but is not plagued with the soot and grime of the northern industrial cities. Instead, it is noted for beer making, electronics, vehicle construction, fashions, printing, film-making, optical and precision instruments, and civil engineering. There are many banks, insurance companies and scientific research institutes. Large commercial exhibits at the Theresienhohe feature crafts, construction machinery and other products of the region.

You will find the people of Bavaria far more relaxed and less formal than the people of northern Germany, and they are proud of the fact. Even their dialect differs; the local greeting, for example, is *Grüss Gott* (God be with you) rather than *Guten Tag*, the greeting in most of Germany. Bavarians are enthusiastic beer drinkers, heavy eaters, and great lovers of music.

Housing
Housing is scarce and accommodation tends to be small, as in most German cities. Most people live in large multiplex apartment buildings or in terraced houses. The public transport system is excellent and consists of the U-bahn, tram and bus service, and the S-bahn, which reaches well beyond city limits. Because this is a large metropolitan area, people tend to consider proximity to schools first (if they have school-age children) and to jobs second when searching for a place to live.

The lists of flats and houses for rent in the Friday edition of the *Süddeutsche Zeitung* and the Saturday edition of the *Münchner Merkur* are the best resources for house or flat hunting. Placing an ad in the flat- or house-wanted sections of those papers is also useful.

Leisure activities
München is a delightful city to explore. The Marienplatz, the heart of the old city, is flanked by the new city hall with its famous *Glockenspiel* (the largest carillon in Germany) and ringed by small streets lined with luxury shops, restaurants and cafés. The magnificent churches located here include St Michael's and the cathedral, both restored after the war. Perhaps the most stunning, certainly the most surprising, is the Church of Our Lady. Severely damaged by bombing, the sober brick facade markedly contrasts with a dazzling white, modern nave and contemporary stained glass windows. Close by is the open market, with beautifully arranged vegetables and flowers, and a street lined with butcher shops from which hang vast quantities of *Wurst*. Of course, there are the great beer halls, the most famous of which is the Hofbrauhaus, with its many rooms and courtyards, and bands playing lively tunes.

Operas and concerts are truly outstanding, and the theatre and ballet equally notable. There is a great variety of important museums and galleries. The Alte Pinakothek, with masterpieces by Rubens, Dürer and Van Dyck, is considered one of the seven most important art galleries in the world. The Neue Pinakothek has an important collection of eighteenth- and nineteenth-century paintings and sculpture. The Deutsches Museum features displays of scientific and technological developments from the Stone Age to the present. The Palace of the Dukes of Wittelsbach (constructed around seven courtyards) and the Palace Museum, Theatre and Opera display the glory of royal life in old München. Churches are mostly Catholic or Lutheran.

Outdoor activities are abundant; there are two public golf courses, tennis courts, swimming pools, skating arenas, bowling centres, and riding clubs. Children enjoy the many parks and the Hellabrün Zoo. Outside München, you can learn mountain climbing in the Isar Valley, ski in Allgau and Werdenfelser, and swim, camp and sail in the Tegernsee, with its charming small towns. The health resort of Bad Tolz is also popular. The S-bahn provides easy access to Lake Starnberg or the Ammersee Lake with Andechs Monastery, where excellent beer is brewed. It is great fun to take a picnic dinner, buy a few litres of beer, and relax in the beer hall or courtyard of Andechs.

München is a great city for celebrating and seems to host a constant round of festivals. *Oktoberfest* is world-renowned, and *Fasching* (carnival) features literally thousands of masked balls. The summer cultural festivities reach their high point with the Opera Festival in July; and, as one foreign resident put it, 'You just haven't celebrated Christmas until you live in Munich'. The city seems to glow in the winter holiday season, and the *Christkindlmarkt* on Marienplatz is a real treat for 'people watchers' as well as a source of both small, inexpensive gifts and ornaments and more expensive craft items.

Useful addresses
British Consulate-General, 8000 München 40, Amalienstrasse 62

Verkehrsamt (Tourist Office), D-8000 München 2, Rindermarkt 5; the Tourist Office has a wealth of information about Munich and will supply useful brochures and maps and, upon request, the 'Official Monthly Programme' by post.

BONN

Although it is the capital city of the Federal Republic of Germany, Bonn is among its smaller cities, with a population of less than 290,000 in its metropolitan area.

Situated twenty miles from Köln, Bonn spreads out on both

banks of the Rhine River and is the gateway to the Rhine Valley. One of the oldest settlements in Germany, its history dates back 2,000 years. Under the name of Castra Bonnensia, Bonn was the site of one of the earliest Roman forts on the Rhine River and an important part of the Romans' defence of the area. It is also the site of one of the first Christian shrines, built to honour the memory of two Roman soldiers, Cassius and Florentius, who were killed because of their belief in Christianity. Today the Bonn cathedral stands on this spot.

In the thirteenth century, the archbishops of Köln established their residence in Bonn and were responsible for the development of the city as it is today. The parks and avenues were laid out, monuments were erected, and the residence itself was constructed. The old and famous University of Bonn was completed in 1725. Also built during this period were Poppelsdorfer Schloss and the city hall. Bonn was selected as the capital of the Federal Republic of Germany in 1949. In June 1991, the Bundestag voted after much debate to move the Parliament and seat of government to Berlin; this move is expected to take about twelve years to complete.

Bad Godesberg, an ancient and well-known spa, is incorporated into the city of Bonn and houses much of the diplomatic community. It is also the birthplace of Beethoven. The house in which he was born in 1770 is now a museum.

Schools
There are British, American and French elementary schools in the area, all of which follow their home-country curriculum. At the elementary level, there are Catholic, Protestant and non-denominational private schools. The Nicolas-Cusanus Gymnasium near the Plittersdorf is one of the few secondary schools prepared to give international students special attention. It is tuition-free and there are special German classes designed to help international students learn the language.

Leisure activities
Bonn is a bustling city—a combination of political, intellectual, cultural and commercial activities abound. Its operas, plays, concerts and festivals are among the best in the country. During *Bonner Sommer*, from the beginning of May until September, concerts, drama and dance are performed on stages in the Markt Platz, the Gartenschau Park, and the Pavilion in Bad Godesberg.

Summer is also the time for concerts at Schloss Bruhl in Köln and in the courtyard of the Poppelsdorfer Schloss.

At the end of summer, wine festivals celebrate the grape harvest. Each village has its own festival featuring dancing to the music of local bands, contest and, most important, wine tasting of last year's local vintage.

Children from two to ninety-two will enjoy the Christkindlmarkt in Münster Platz. From late November until Christmas it features booths full of sweets, wooden ornaments and handcrafts. It is a great source of small and inexpensive gifts.

Religious services are conducted in English at the St Boniface Anglican Church and at the Christian Science Church. Protestant, Catholic and Jewish services are available in German.

Activity and enrichment groups exist for almost every age group and every interest. The *Bonn Journal* is the best source of information on the activities of the various groups as well as for information on concerts, art exhibits and special events.

German Tourist Information Centres

These are the principal German tourist information centres:

Deutsche Zentrale für Tourismus e.V.
(Federal German Tourist Board)
Beethovenst. 69
D-6000 Frankfurt 1
Tel (069) 7572-0

Deutsche Fremdenverkehrsverband
e.V.
(German Tourist Association)
Niebuhrstr. 16b
D-5300 Bonn 1

Berlin Tourist Information
30, Europa Center
D-1000 Berlin 12

Informationszentrum Berlin
Hardenbergst. 20
D-1000 Berlin 12

Verkehrsverein der Freien Hansestadt
Bremen
Bahnhofspl. 29
D-2800 Bremen 1

Landesverkehrsverband Westfalen
e.V.
Südwall 6
D-4600 Dortmund

Hamburg Information GmbH
Postfach 10 27 23
Burchardst. 14
D-2000 Hamburg 1

Fremdenverkehrsverband
Schleswig-Holstein
Niemannsweg 31
D-2300 Kiel 1

Fremdenverkehrsverband
Rheinland-Pfalz
Postfach 1420
Löhrst. 103-105
D-5400 Koblenz

Landesfremdenverkehrsverband
Bayern e.V.
Prinzregentenstr. 18/IV
D-8000 München 22

Fremdenverkehrsverband Saarland e.V.
Postfach 242
Am Stiefel 2
D-6600 Saarbrücken 3

Landesverkehrsverband
Baden-Württemberg e.V.
Bussenstr. 23
D-7000 Stuttgart

Fremdenverkehrsverband Hessen e.V.
Abraham-Lincoln-Str. 38-42
D-6200 Wiesbaden

Appendix
Social Security

SOCIAL SECURITY, HEALTH CARE AND PENSION RIGHTS IN THE EUROPEAN COMMUNITY

The Federal Republic of Germany is a member of the **European Community**, along with the UK, Belgium, Denmark, France, Gibraltar, Greece, the Republic of Ireland, Italy, Luxembourg, the Netherlands, Portugal and Spain.

European Community Regulations give equal treatment and protection of benefit rights to employed and self-employed people who are EC citizens, and to their dependants.

WILL I CONTINUE TO BE COVERED BY THE UK NATIONAL INSURANCE SCHEME?

If you work in another EC country for an EC employer (which includes a UK employer) or are self-employed:

- generally you will be insured under the Social Security legislation of the country in which you work (see below for provisions in Germany):
- usually there will be no liability for UK National Insurance contributions.

There are, however, **exceptions** to the above general rules.

1. If your employer in the UK sends you to work in another EC country for a period not expected to be more than 12 months, you will normally continue to be subject to the UK National Insurance scheme. Your employer must obtain a certificate (**form E101**) from the Department of Social Security (DSS),

Overseas Branch, Newcastle-upon-Tyne NE98 1YX. As soon as you arrive in your new country, this certificate should be presented to the local social security office in order to establish exemption from joining that country's scheme.

2. If your employment unexpectedly lasts longer than 12 months, it is possible to apply to remain insured under the UK scheme for a further period of not more than 12 months (**form E102**). Your employer must apply before the end of the first 12 month period.

3. If you are self-employed in the UK and go to work in another country for a period not expected to be more than 12 months, you will continue to be subject to the UK National Insurance scheme (**form E101**, as above).

Note: Special provisions apply if you are employed or self-employed in two or more EC countries, or if you are self-employed in one EC country and employed in another.

For full details, see leaflet SA29, issued by the Department of Social Security and obtainable from local DSS offices.

Child benefit
If you are insured as an employed or self-employed person under the UK scheme while in another EC country, UK child benefit will normally be payable for your children even if they are living in another EC country.

If you become insured as an employed or self-employed person under the scheme of another EC country, that country's children's allowance will normally be payable even though your children remain in the UK. Your previous UK insurance contributions may be taken into account to help you satisfy the other country's conditions for children's allowance.

If you and your spouse could both qualify for benefit for the same child from two different EC countries, both countries will *not* have to pay their benefit in full.

If you need further information about Child Benefit, write to: Department of Social Security, Child Benefit Centre (Washington), Newcastle upon Tyne, NE88 1AA.

Health care

In order to receive sickness benefits and medical treatment in another EC country, you will normally need to have made contributions under that country's insurance scheme. The UK will not be responsible for the payment of any medical treatment received in another EC country, unless you have remained under the UK National Insurance scheme under the provisions outlined above. If you are entitled to payment of medical costs, you should obtain a certificate (**form E111**) available from post offices or from the DSS Overseas Branch (see above).

Unemployment benefit

If you are getting UK Unemployment Benefit and have been registered as available for work (normally for 4 weeks) at a UK Unemployment Benefit office, you may continue to receive benefit for up to 3 months while you look for work elsewhere in the EC, provided you are getting benefit at your date of departure.

If you are going to Germany to look for work, a certificate of authorisation (**form E303**) will be issued to you provided you give the Unemployment Benefit office sufficient notice of your departure, otherwise it will be sent to your address in that country.

You must register for work and follow the new country's procedures for claiming benefit.

In Germany you should register at the *Arbeitsamt* (Employment Office) in the Department for Jobfinding Advice (*Abteilung AV/ AB*). You should request form '*Antrag auf Arbeitslosengeld*' and ask for the address of the office to which you should take this form.

(For further advice, see leaflet UBL 22, obtainable from local Unemployment Benefit offices.)

SOCIAL SECURITY PROVISIONS IN GERMANY

All employees in a German establishment of whatever nationality, and their dependants, automatically become members of the Federal Republic's social security system (unless the foreigner is from another EC country and his employment will probably last less than 12 months—see above). The local social security office needs to be informed immediately you take up your employment in Germany.

Contributions

Health, accident, pension and unemployment insurance are financed from contributions. (Child allowances are paid out of taxes.)

One-half of the contributions towards health, pension and unemployment insurance are paid by the employer, the other half by the employee. The employer bears the whole cost of the accident insurance scheme.

Health insurance

The health insurance scheme covers the following:

- Costs of treatment (including health maintenance and preventive care)
- Income maintenance
- Maternity benefits
- Household maintenance
- Death benefits

The scheme is compulsory for all employed persons (except for salaried staff with earnings above the statutory limits—who may, however, remain in the statutory scheme on a voluntary basis).

Health insurance protection is guaranteed by local health insurance offices (*Allgemeine Ortskrankenkassen—AOK*), company insurance offices (*Betriebskrankenkassen—BKK*) and trade insurance offices (*Innungskrankenkassen—IKK*) as well as by semi-private health insurance schemes (*Ersatzkassen*) and by the miners' benefit fund (*Knappschaftskasse*). Your employer will be able to tell you which local health office is legally responsible and what opportunities there are to join a company or semi-private scheme.

All dependants are covered by the same scheme and enjoy the same benefits, provided they normally live in the Federal Republic.

Medical treatment

Treatment by doctors, specialists and dentists is provided free of charge to all insured persons and their dependants. An insurance certificate (*Krankenschein*) must be produced when treatment is needed. The certificate can be obtained from your sickness fund or your employer.

You can choose your own doctor from the list of doctors licensed to treat members of public health insurance schemes (as almost all doctors are licensed, you have a wide choice).

Prescription charges
Patients over the age of 16 must pay a small set charge for prescribed medicines.

Hospital treatment
The insurance scheme covers the costs of hospital treatment, including medicines. People over the age of 18 have to pay a small daily share of costs, which is charged for 14 days at the most in each year.

In certain cases, e.g. where a child under 8 has to be taken care of, a 'house helper' may be allocated to help maintain the household during the time when someone is in hospital.

Sickness benefits
If an employee is unable to work because of illness or accident, the employer will normally continue to pay that person's wages for 6 weeks. After that, the insurance scheme will pay sickness benefit (*Krankengeld*) amounting to 80 per cent of net pay (benefits are tax free).

Sickness benefit is also payable if an employee has to take time off work to care for a sick child under 8 years of age. This benefit is payable for up to 5 days per year per child.

Accident insurance
All employers are members of the industrial safety authority (*Berufsgenossenschaft*) responsible for their particular branch of industry. Employees are insured against industrial accidents arising out of their employment, including occupational illnesses.

Accident insurance also covers school children during attendance at school, and students undergoing vocational or advanced training.

Pension schemes
All employees, regardless of their level of earnings, and including foreign workers, are compulsorily insured in the appropriate insurance scheme as soon as they enter employment. The pension schemes are administered by the *Land* insurance agencies (*Landesversicherungsanstalten*) for wage-earners and by the Federal Insurance Agency (*Bundesversicherungsanstalten*) for salaried

employees. There are no differences between the two schemes as regards contribution rates or benefits.

Self-employed people and housewives can pay voluntary contributions to the scheme in order to provide for a retirement pension.

Benefits
The pension insurance schemes cover:

- occupational disability pensions
- working disability pensions
- benefits for single parents
- retirement pensions
- survivors' pensions

Company pension schemes
Over half the employees in Germany are covered by company pension schemes which provide disability, old-age and survivors' pensions over and above the statutory scheme.

Unemployment benefits
Unemployment benefits (*Arbeitslosengeld*) are paid to unemployed persons who have completed the 'waiting period' and are available when required by the labour exchange.

An unemployed person is defined as someone who is employed for not more than 20 hours per week. He or she must be capable of employment under normal labour market conditions.

The 'waiting period' had been complied with if the person has been employed and paid insurance contributions for not less than 360 days during the past three years.

The level of benefits is based on previous net wages, and the length of time for which benefits are payable depends on the length of employment during the previous three years.

Unemployment assistance
Unemployment assistance (*Arbeitslosenhilfe*) is payable to unemployed people who are not eligible for unemployment benefit and are not able to support themselves by any other means. Levels of benefit are generally lower than unemployment benefit.

Registration

As soon as you become unemployed you should contact your employment office (*Arbeitsamt*) and ask for information on all rules and formalities to be complied with for the award and payment of benefits. In particular, you must:

- report to the employment office when asked to do so;
- not refuse a job offered without valid reasons;
- notify the office of any changes in your circumstances.

Insurance documents

As soon as you begin work, your employer will take the necessary steps to have you registered for insurance with the sickness insurance fund (*Krankenkasse*), which will then inform the relevant pension and unemployment insurance bodies. You will be allocated an insurance number under which the pension insurance institution will record your period of insurance and your earnings on which you will have to pay contributions.

The pension insurance institution will send you an insurance book (*Versicherungsnachweisheft*). You should take your insurance identity card (*Ausweis*) from the insurance book and hand the book to your employer straight away.

Children's allowances

All employed and self-employed people having their permanent or ordinary residence in the Federal Republic, including foreign nationals, receive children's allowances (*Kindergeld*) for their dependant children. It is granted on a uniform basis, graduated according to the number of children and beginning with the first child.

Allowances are generally payable for children under the age of 16, and for older children up to the age of 27 if they are still at school or undergoing vocational training.

Children's allowances are paid every two months by the local employment office (*Arbeitsamt*). You must apply for them on a form which you can obtain from the employment office. Ask for '*Antrag auf Kindergeld für ausländische Arbeitnehmer*'.

Note: More detailed information about Germany's social security provisions can be found in a booklet, *Social Security for Migrant Workers—Federal Republic of Germany*, available from the Department of Social Security, Overseas Branch, Newcastle-upon-Tyne NE98 1YX.

Glossary

SOCIAL OCCASIONS

Abendbrot ('Evening bread') Informal meal
Abendessen ('Evening meal') More formal meal
Auf Wiedersehen Goodbye
Bitte Please/you are welcome
Danke Thank you
Grüss Gott God be with you (greeting in Bavaria)
Guten Abend Good evening
Guten Morgen Good morning
Gute Nacht Goodnight
Guten Tag Good day/Hello/How do you do
Kaffeeklatsch Social gathering to drink coffee and chat with friends
Prosit! Good health/cheers!
Zum Wohl! To your health/cheers!

EMPLOYMENT AND BUSINESS

Abteilungsleiter Head of department
Aktiengesellschaft (AG) Joint stock company
Arbeitsamt Employment office
Arbeitslosengeld Unemployment benefit
Arbeitslosenhilfe Unemployment assistance
Aufenthaltserlaubnis Residence permit
Aufsichtsrat Supervisory board of business/company
Betriebsrat Works council
Bundesanstalt für Arbeit Federal Labour Office
Deutscher Gewerkschaftsbund (DGB) German Union Federation

Gastarbeiter Guest (i.e. foreign) worker
Generalbevollmächtigter General manager
Krankengeld Sickness benefit
Krankenkasse Health insurance
i.v. (in Vollmacht) With authority (to negotiate, etc.)
p.p.a. (Prokurist) Manager with registered signing authority (corporate secretary)
Stellvertretender Vorsitz Deputy Chairman
Voritzer/Vorsitzender Chairman
Vorstand Board of management

HOUSING

Kaution Deposit against damage
Leere Wohnung Unfurnished flat
Möblierte Wohnung Furnished flat
Möblierte Zimmer Furnished room
Wohnungsamt Housing office

OFFICES, SHOPS AND RESTAURANTS

Apotheke Chemist's shop (prescription drugs)
Ausländeramt Aliens Authority
Bäckerei Baker's shop
Bedienung Service charge
Briefmarken Postage stamps
Buchhandlung Bookshop
Drogerei Chemist's shop (non-prescription drugs, cosmetics, etc.)
Feinkost Delicatessen
Fleischerei Butcher's shop
Gasthaus Guesthouse
Gasthof Inn
Gaststätte Restaurant/pub
Geldwechsel Foreign exchange office
Kaufhaus Department store
Lebensmittelgeschäft Grocer's
Metzgerei Butcher's shop
Obst- und Gemüseladen Greengrocer's
Postamt Post office
Postwertzeichen Postage stamps
Rathaus Town hall
Sonderangebot Special offer, reduced price

Spielwaren Toyshop
Tabakwarenladen Tobacconist's
Verkehrsamt Local tourist office
Wechselstube Foreign exchange office
Zimmernachweis Accommodation information office

TRANSPORT AND COMMUNICATIONS

Bedarfshaltestelle Request stop (buses and trams)
Bushaltestelle Bus stop
D-Zug Express train
E-Zug Stopping train
Ferngespräch Trunk call (telephone)
Gelbe Seiten Yellow pages
Haltestelle Tram stop
Hauptbahnhof Main railway station
IC-Zug Inter city train
Ortsgespräch Local telephone call
Personenzug Local train
U-bahn (Untergrundbahn) Underground railway
Vorwahlen Area codes (telephone)

Further Reading

GENERAL

Ardagh, John, *Germany and the Germans* (Hamish Hamilton 1987)
Craig, Gordon A., *The Germans* (Penguin 1990)
James, Harold, *German Identity 1770-1990* (Weidenfeld & Nicolson 1990)
Mellor, *Two Germanies: A Modern Geography* (Harper & Row 1978)

HISTORY

Eley, Geoff, *From Unification to Nazism: Reinterpreting the German Past* (Allen & Unwin 1985)
Gorman, Michael, *The Unification of Germany 1815-1866* (Cambridge University Press 1989)
Haffner, Sebastian, *Germany's Self-Destruction: From Bismarck to Hitler* (Simon & Shuster 1989)
Kershaw, Ian, *The Nazi Dictatorship: Problems and Perspectives of Interpretation* (Edward Arnold 1985)
Mann, Golo, *The History of Germany Since 1789* (Penguin 1985)
Richardson, Nigel, *The Third Reich* (Dryad 1987)
Shirer, William L., *The Rise and Fall of the Third Reich* (Hamlyn 1987)
Taylor, A.J.P., *The Course of German History: A Survey of the Development of German History Since 1815* (Routledge 1988)
Turner, Henry Ashby, *The Two Germanies Since 1945* (Yale University Press 1989)

ART AND LITERATURE

Elsaesser, *New German Cinema: A History* (Macmillan 1989)

Garland & Garland, eds., *Oxford Companion to German Literature* (Oxford University Press, 2nd edition 1986)
German Art Now (Design Profile Series) (Academy Editions 1989)
Gray, Ronald, *German Tradition in Literature 1871-1945* (Cambridge University Press 1977)
Hamburger, *German Poetry 1910-75* (Carcanet 1977)
Rentschler, *German Film and Literature* (Methuen 1986)
Whitford, Frank, *Bauhaus*, (Art School) (Thames & Hudson 1984)

POLITICS, ECONOMICS AND SOCIAL STUDIES

Berghahn, Volker R., *Modern Germany: Society, Economy and Politics in the Twentieth Century* (Cambridge University Press 1987)
Broszat, Martin, *Hitler and the Collapse of Weimar Germany* (Berg 1987)
Hughes, Michael, *Nationalism and Society: Germany 1800-1945* (Edward Arnold 1988)
Marsh, David, *New Germany: At the Crossroads* (Century 1990)
Morton, Edwina, ed., *Germany between East and West* (Cambridge University Press 1987)
Stern, Fritz, *Gold and Iron: Bismarck, Bleichroder and the Building of the German Reich* (Penguin 1987)
Wehler, Hans-Ulrich, *The German Empire 1871-1918* (Berg 1985)

EAST GERMANY

Dennis, Mike, *German Democratic Republic (1953-1987): Politics, Economics and Society* (Pinter 1988)
McCauley, Martin, *The German Democratic Republic Since 1945* (University of London 1986)
Sharman, Tim, *We Live in East Germany* (Wayland 1985)
Simmons, Michael, *The Unloved Country: A Portrait of East Germany Today* (Abacus 1989)

WEST GERMANY

Koch, Karl, ed., *West Germany Today* (Routledge 1989)
Smith, Gordon, *Democracy in Western Germany: Parties and Politics in the Federal Republic* (Gower 1985)

BERLIN

Clare, George, *Berlin Days 1946-47* (Pan Books 1990)
Dudman, John, *The Division of Berlin* (Wayland 1987)
Gelb, Norman, *The Berlin Wall* (Joseph 1986)
Jackson, Robert, *The Berlin Airlift 1945-1949* (P. Stephens 1988)
Kemp, Anthony, *Escape from Berlin* (Boxtree 1987)
Simmons, Michael, *Berlin: The Dispossessed City* (Hamish Hamilton 1988)
Tusa, Ann, *The Berlin Blockade* (Coronet 1989)
Waldenburg, *Berlin Wall Book* (Thames & Hudson 1990)
Walker, Ian, *Zoo Station: Adventures in East and West Berlin* (Abacus 1988)

LAW

Horn, *An Introduction to German Private and Commercial Law* (Oxford University Press 1982)
Gres & Jung, *German Employment Law* (Kluwer Law & Taxation Publishers 1983)
Oliver, *Private Company in Germany* (Kluwer Law & Taxation Publishers 1986)

TRAVEL

Aldridge, Janet, *West Germany* (Off the Beaten Track—Visitors' Guide) (MPC 1989)
Bentley, James, *Germany* (Blue Guide) (A & C Black 1987)
Berlin Transit: A Travel Guide 1986-7 (Thomas Cook 1986)
Berlitz Travel Guide to Berlin (Berlitz Guides 1987)
Bernhard, Marianne, *Baedeker's AA Berlin* (Automobile Association 1984)
Dornberg, J., ed., *Penguin Guide to Germany* (Penguin 1990)
Fodor ed., *Germany 1990* (Fodor's Travel Publications 1990)
Germany (Automobile Association 1981)
Hoefer, *Berlin* (Harrap 1989)
Hoefer ed., *Germany* (Insight Guides) (Harrap 1988)
Holland Rough Guide to Berlin (Harrap Columbus 1990)
Mehling, *Germany* (Cultural Guides) (Phaidon Press 1985)
Phillips, John A. S., *Coping with Germany* (Basil Blackwell 1989)

Phillips, John A. S., *Long Stays in Germany* (David & Charles 1990)
Steves, Rick, *Germany, Austria & Switzerland in Your Pocket* (Horizon 1989)
Walker, John, *Footloose in Berlin: The Berlin You Might Have Missed* (T. Reed 1988)

FOOD AND DRINK

Brown, Karen, *German Country Inns and Castles* (Harrap Columbus 1989)
Howe, Robin, *German Cooking* (Deutsch 1983)
Johnson, Hugh, *Atlas of German Wines and Traveller's Guide to the Vineyards* (Mitchell Beazley 1986)
Little German Cook Book (Appletree Press 1990)
Garcia, *Traveller's Guide to the German Menu* (Absolute Press 1985)

GOVERNMENT PUBLICATIONS

Focus Germany: A Profile of the Federal Republic of Germany and West Berlin (British Overseas Trade Board, 1987)
Hints to Exporters: Federal Republic of Germany and West Berlin (British Overseas Trade Board 1990)
West Germany: List of Export Marketing Consultants (British Overseas Trade Board 1990)
West Germany: Solicitors Conversant with German Law (British Overseas Trade Board 1990)
Your Social Security, Health Care and Pension Rights in the European Community (Leaflet SA 29, Department of Social Security)

PUBLICATIONS OF THE GOVERNMENT OF THE FEDERAL REPUBLIC OF GERMANY

Press and Information Office Leaflets:
   14 *Higher Education*
   15 *The Education System*
   23 *Public Health*
   28 *Vocational Training*
Information Booklet no. 119 for Migrant Workers (Bundesverwaltungsamt—Federal Office of Administration)

EUROPEAN COMMUNITY PUBLICATIONS

Social Security for Migrant Workers: FR of Germany (Office for Official Publications of the European Communities 1985)
The European Community publishes many reports, surveys and other studies. To obtain a full list of materials, write to the Commission of the European Communities, 22 rue de la Loi, B-1049 Brussels; or the Office for Official Publications of the European Communities, Batiment Jean Monnet, L-2985 Luxembourg.

ORGANISATION FOR ECONOMIC COOPERATION AND DEVELOPMENT (OECD)

The OECD is another source of abundant documentation, for example *OECD Economic Survey: Federal Republic of West Germany*. Publications can be obtained from the headquarters in Bonn: OECD Publications and Information Centre, D.5300 Bonn, Simrackstrasse 4, Federal Republic of Germany.

BANK PUBLICATIONS

ABECOR Country Report: Federal Republic of Germany, Barclays Bank Group, Economic Intelligence Unit, 54 Lombard Street, London EC3P 3AH.
Economic Report: The Federal Republic of Germany, Lloyds Bank Group Economics Department, 71 Lombard Street, London EC3P 3BS.
Spotlight West Germany, Midland Bank International, 110 Cannon Street, London EC4N 6AA.
Federal Republic of Germany (Overseas Economic Reports series), National Westminster Bank plc, 41 Lothbury, London EC2P 2BP.

Useful Addresses

Allgemeiner Deutscher Automobil Club (ADAC), D.8000 München 22, Königstrasse 9-11A, Federal Republic of Germany

Anglo-German Association, 17 Bloomsbury Square, London WC1A 2LP (Tel: 071 831 8696). Subscription for single members £10, for married couples £16. Has a full programme of events including a Youth Programme.

Anglo-German Club, PO Box 427, London W8 5QU. A club for young people. Contact Anabel Meikle, enclosing s.a.e.

Association of Translators and Interpreters (BDU—Bundesverband der Dolmetscher und Ubersetzer e.V.) 4100 Duisburg, Mulheimerstrasse (Tel: 357-480)

Automobilclub von Deutschland (AVD), D.6000 Frankfurt-Niederrad, Lyonerstrasse 16, Federal Republic of Germany

British Chamber of Commerce in Germany (BCCG), D.5000 Köln 1, Heumarkt 14, Federal Republic of Germany

British Consulates-General:
- 1000 Berlin 12, Uhlandstrasse 7-8, Federal Republic of Germany (Tel: 030 309 5295/7)
- 4000 Düsseldorf 30, Georg-Glock-Strasse 14, Federal Republic of Germany (Tel: 0211 43740)
- 6000 Frankfurt am Main, Bockenheimer Landstrasse 51-53, Federal Republic of Germany (Tel: 069 720406/9)
- 2000 Hamburg 13, Harvestehuderweg 8a, Federal Republic of Germany (Tel: 04044 60 71)
- 8000 München 40, Amalienstrasse 62, Federal Republic of Germany (Tel: 08939 40 15/9)

British Council, 10 Spring Gardens, London SW1A 2BN (Can give advice on recognition of UK qualifications overseas)

British Embassy in Germany, 5300 Bonn 1, Friedrich Ebert Allee 77, Federal Republic of Germany (Tel: 0228 23 40 61)

British Embassy Preparatory School, D.5300 Bonn 2, Bad-Godesburg-Heiderhof, Tulpenbaumweg, Federal Republic of Germany

British High School (Bonn), D.5300 Bonn 2, Gotenstrasse 50, Federal Republic of Germany

British Overseas Trade Board, Germany Desk, Room 374, 1 Victoria Street, London SW1H oLT

Council of British Independent Schools in the European Communities (COBISEC), c/o the British School of Brussels, Chaussée de Louvain, Tervuren, B1980 Belgium (Tel: 32 2 767 47 00)

Department of Social Security, Overseas Branch, Newcastle upon Tyne, NE98 1YX

Deutscher Touring Automobil Club (DTC), D.8000 München 60, Elisabethstrasse 30, Federal Republic of Germany

Deutsches Jugendhergerbswerk Hauptverband (Youth Hostel Association), D-4930 Detmold, Bülowstrasse 26, Federal Republic of Germany

Employment Service, Overseas Placing Unit (OPS 5), c/o Moorfoot, Sheffield S1 4PQ (Offers advice and guidance to people who want to work overseas)

Export Credits Guarantee Department, Export House, 50 Ludgate Hill, London EC4M 7AY

European Council of International Schools (ECIS), 21B Lavant Street, Petersfield, Hampshire GU32 2EL (Tel: 0730 68244) (Publishes a *Directory of International Schools*)

German Academic Exchange Service, 17 Bloomsbury Square London WC1 (Tel: 071-404-4065); 5300 Bonn 2, Kennedyallee 50, Federal Republic of Germany

German Airlines Lufthansa, 28 Piccadilly, London W1 (Tel: 071-408-0322; 071-408-0422)

German Broadcasting, 10 Great Chapel Street, London W1 (Tel: 071-439-7460)

German Chamber of Industry and Commerce in the UK, 12 Suffolk Street, London SW1Y 4HQ (Tel: 071-930-7251)

German Embassy of the Federal Republic of Germany, 23 Belgrave Square, London SW1X 8PZ (Tel: 071-235-5033)

German Golf Association, 6202 Wiesbaden Biebrich, Rheinblickstrasse 24, Federal Republic of Germany

German National Tourist Office, Nightingale House, 65 Curzon Street, London W1 (Tel: 071-495-3990)

German Rail Passenger Services, 18 Conduit Street, London W1 (Tel: 071-499-0577)
German Travel Bureau (DER), 18 Conduit Street, London W1 (Tel: 071-408-0111)
German Tribune, Friedrich Reinecke Verlag GmbH, D-2000 Hamburg 76, Schöne Aussicht 23, Federal Republic of Germany
Goethe Institut, 50 Princes Gate, Exhibition Road, London SW7 2PH. Tel: 071 225 3449. The German cultural organisation which provides German language classes and other facilities.
Inland Revenue Claims Branch, Foreign Division, Merton Road, Bootle L69 9BL
Institute of Linguists, 24a Highbury Grove, London N5 2EA
Institute of Translating and Interpreting, 318a Finchley Road, London NW3 5HT
Simplification of International Trade Procedures Board (SITPRO), Almack House, 26 King Street, London SW1W 6QY
Verband der Deutschen Sportsfischer (German Fishing Association) 605 Offenbach, Bahnhofstrasse 37, Federal Republic of Germany
Verband Deutscher Gebirgs- und Wandervereine e.V. (Association of German Mountain and Touring Clubs), D-2700 Stuttgart 1, Hospitalstrasse 21b, Federal Republic of Germany

Index

Accident insurance, 125
Air service, 43
Aliens Authority, 29
Appliances, electrical, 74
Au pair, 78
Autobahns, 99, 108
Automobile Clubs, 101

Banking, 37, 39
Bavaria, 10
Beer, 81
Beverages, 81
Bonn, 117
Bremen, 10, 109
Bremerhaven, 10, 109
British Chamber of Commerce, 66, 103
Bundesrat, 16
Bundestag, 16
Business
    Entertaining, 64
    Services for UK businesses, 65
    Style, 63

Camping, 108
Canals, 11
Cars
    Importing, 30, 100
    Renting, 100
Characteristics, German, 14
Child benefit, 122
Children's allowancs, 127
Churches, 26
Cinema, 106
Climate, 11
Climbing, 105
Clothes, 32
Clothes, sizes, 82
Commercial representatives, 68
Company organisation, 67
Conscientiousness, 50
Conversation, 57
Credit cards, 37
Culture, 15
Currency, 36

Customs regulations, 29
Customs, social, 55

Dialling codes, 42
Driving regulations, 101
Düsseldorf, 9, 10, 111

East Germans, 19, 22
Economy, 24
Electricity, 74
Employment, 32
European Community, 15, 18, 122
Exporting to Germany, 65

Famous Germans, 15
Federal Institute for Labour, 32
Fishing, 105
Formality, 49, 51
Frankfurt, 9, 10, 112
Friendship, 50

Gastarbeiter (guest workers), 14
Geography, 9
Goethe Institut, 96
Golf, 105
Government, 16

Hamburg, 10
Handshaking, 52
Health care, 84, 123
Health insurance, 25, 84, 123, 124
Hiking, 105
History, 15
Holidays, 39
Hostelling, 104
House purchase, 74
House rules, 73
Household goods, import of, 29, 30
Household help, 78
Housing, 71, 109, 113, 116

Insurance documents, 127
Intellect, respect for, 50
International Baccalaureate, 92
Invitations, 55

Kindergarten, 89

Language, German, 46, 62, 78-80
Leases, 73
Leisure, 103

Magazines, 46
Manners, 53
Measurements, metric, 82
Meat, cuts of, 79
München (Munich), 10, 115
Music, 107

National Insurance, UK, 122
Newspapers, 46
Nightlife, 58
Numbers, German, 39

Passport, 28
Pension schemes, 25, 125
Pension schemes, company, 126
Pets, import of, 30, 31
Politics, 17
Polytechnics, 94
Population, 9, 14, 21
Post offices, 37, 45
Postal Savings Account, 35
Postal Service, 44
Privacy, 50, 64
Promptness, 54
Public holidays, 39

Rabies, 31
Radio, 45, 47
Reading, 107
Religion, 26
Renting, 72
Residence permit, 28
Rhine, 11
Rhineland, 10
Road signs, 100
Ruhr, 10

Sailing, 105
Schools
  American, 91
  Choice of, 86
  English language, 90
  German, 89
  Primary, 87
  Secondary, 87
Shoes, 32
Shopping, 39, 47, 78
Shops
  Opening hours, 80
  Sales, 80
  Speciality, 78
Social security, 14, 128
Spas, 10, 85
Speed limits, 99
Sports, 104
Studying in Germany, 94
Summer schools, 97

Tax Card, 28
Taxes, 37
Taxes, Church, 26
Taxis, 38
Telephone, 43
Telephone installation, 75
Television, 45, 47
Theatre, 106
Time, German, 38
Tipping, 38
Titles, 51
Toasts, 56
Tourist information centres, 120
Trade Unions, 25
Trains, 43
Transport, 41
Travel, 107

Underground railways, 41
Unemployment, 25
Unemployment benefits, 25, 123, 126
Unification, 14, 18, 19
Universities, 71, 94

Values, 50
VAT, 38

Walking, 105
Wine, 81
Work camps, 33
Worker participation, 25

Yellow Pages, 44
Youth hostels, 75-76, 104

Other titles in this series:

How to Live & Work in Belgium
Marvina Shilling

Researched and written by a specialist on Belgian affairs, this is a complete manual of essential information on Belgium from entering the country to taking up residence, coping with the language, living in Brussels, Antwerp and other major cities, understanding the business, official and legal environment, the cost of living and other vital facts and advice for executives, officials, technicians, students, teachers and others.
128pp illus. 0 7463 0564 8

How to Live & Work in France
Nicole Prevost Logan

This book meets the need for a clear compendium of information and advice for longer-stay visitors or residents, whether their interests are commercial, official, technical, educational or lifestyle/retirement. It includes an extensive contacts section covering embassies and consulates, travel contacts, business contacts (including banks) in both Britain and France, and miscellaneous key addresses. An extensive further reading section lists more than 100 books and periodicals. Nicole Prevost Logan was born in France. She became licensed in Law at the University of Paris and obtained the Diploma in Political Science from the Institut D'Etudes Politiques. An experienced teacher, cultural adviser and student counsellor, she presently teaches French language and civilisation.
160pp illus. 0 7463 0516 8

How to Live & Work in Spain
Robert A C Richards

Witten by a British expatriate who has lived and worked in Spain for more than 25 years, this new book provides a user-friendly guide for everyone planning to live in Spain on a temporary or permanent basis, and whether for business, professional purposes, study, leisure or retirement. Written with gusto, the book gives a fascinating warts'n'all account of Spain's variegated lifestyles and how to cope.
160pp illus. 1 85703 011 7

How to Get a Job Abroad
Roger Jones BA(Hons) DipEd DPA
Second Edition

This popular title is essential reading for everyone planning to spend a period abroad. A key feature is the lengthy reference section of medium and long-term job opportunities and possibilities, arranged by region and country of the world, and by profession/occupation. There are more than 130 pages of specific contracts and leads, giving literally hundreds of addresses and much hard-to-find information. There is a classified guide to overseas recruitment agencies, and even a multi-lingual guide to writing application letters. 'A fine book for anyone considering even a temporary overseas job.' *The Evening Star.* 'A highly informative and well researched book . . . containing lots of hard information and a first class reference section . . . A superb buy.' *The Escape Committee Newsletter.* Roger Jones BA AKC DipTESL DipEd MInstAM DPA MBIM has himself worked abroad for many years and is a specialist writer on expatriate and employment matters. 288pp illus. 1 85703 003 6. 2nd edition

How to Study Abroad
Teresa Tinsley BA DipEd

Studying abroad can open up a whole new horizon of opportunities, but what courses are available? How does one qualify? What does it cost? Can anyone do it? This new book brings together a wealth of fascinating advice and reference information for everyone who has dreamed of pursuing a course of studies abroad, from art and archaeology to languages, music, science and technology.
160pp illus. 0 7463 0340 8

How to Teach Abroad
Roger Jones BA(Hons) DipEd DPA

'An excellent book . . . An exhaustive and practical coverage of the possibilities and practicalities of teaching overseas.' *The Escape Committee Newsletter.*
176pp illus. 0 7463 0551 6